Extended Schools

A guide to making it work

Suzanne O'Connell
and Julia Everitt

continuum

Continuum International Publishing Group

The Tower Building
11 York Road
London
SE1 7NX

80 Maiden Lane,
Suite 704
New York,
NY 10038

www.continuumbooks.com

British Library Cataloguing-in-Publication Data
A catalogue record for this book is available from the British Library.

ISBN: 9781855397521 (paperback)

Library of Congress Cataloging-in-Publication Data
O'Connell, Suzanne.
Extended schools : a guide to making it work / Suzanne O'Connell and
Julia Everett.
p. cm.
ISBN 978-1-85539-752-1 (pbk.)
1. Community and school. 2. Educational change. 3.
Interorganizational relations. I. Everett, Julia. II. Title.

LC215.O26 2010
370.19—dc22

Typeset by Ben Cracknell Studios | www.benstudios.co.uk
Printed and bound in Great Britain by Bell & Bain Ltd, Glasgow

A companion website to accompany this book is available online at: http://education.oconnell.continuumbooks.com

Please visit the link and register with us to receive your password and to access these downloadable resources.

If you experience any problems accessing the resources, please contact Continuum at: info@continuumbooks.com

Also available from Continuum

Schools and Communities, John West-Burnham, Maggie Farrar and George Otero

Contents

Figures, tables and resources

Figures

Tables

Online resources

1 What is an extended school anyway?

> We will create 'extended' schools in the most deprived areas. These schools will be able to provide a range of services for children, their families and the wider community – including childcare, study support, adult and family learning, access to modern technology, health and social care – working closely with local health and other services and voluntary bodies. (DfES, 2002b: 29)

How it used to be

At one time schools were not extended at all. Imagine Jane Eyre's school, Lowood, opening itself up to family learning? Families had little interest or inclination in finding out what progress their children made or how they might help them at home. Equally, schools had no interest in involving the parents and certainly not the wider community. School was school and home was home. For many families it was just a holding point between birth and employment – and the sooner they were earning the better.

The aims of many schools were barely educational. Their mission was often something very different from the standards agenda we see now. Board schools were rescuing children from parental decadence and church schools from moral decadence. There was an inbuilt assumption that schools were the fount of all knowledge, albeit knowledge of little use in the real world and of scant practical value.

But things have changed and expectations are that schools have an open door (behind the CCTV) and welcome us in. There is growing recognition that parents and communities have a tremendous amount of influence on young people and that schools have relatively little. Therefore, to improve results and to address social issues we must extend our landscape. Parents and the wider community are at last being recognized as an intrinsic part of what schools do. Or try to.

A growing involvement

The kind of thinking that includes parents and the wider community is not completely new. There have always been those who saw a different vision for schools within their communities. Henry Morris in the 1920s developed 'village colleges' in Cambridgeshire as a way of regenerating rural areas. He saw the fast rate at which society was changing and how individuals and families were finding it difficult to adapt. The village colleges were designed to serve social, cultural, educational and economic ends whilst breaking down the barriers between these different parts of people's lives.

Since Henry Morris there have been intermittent drives to develop the school within its community. In 1949, Stewart Mason proposed that community colleges be developed in Leicestershire. An early exponent of consultation, he believed that local people should decide what these colleges should offer. Geoff Cooksey, Director of Stantonbury Campus in Milton Keynes, opened the gates for 20 hours a day every day of the week and offered a whole range of facilities, including a leisure centre, a youth centre, church, shops and theatre. Staff moved flexibly between the different sectors and there was close collaboration between the facilities.

These individuals are just a small sample of those with outstanding vision and a capacity to fulfil it well ahead of their times. It took a lot longer for legislation to catch up.

The Plowden Report 'Children and Their Primary Schools' (1967) was groundbreaking not only in terms of its recognition of the importance of parents but also in its recommendation that schools should be used by the wider community:

> School buildings and grounds represent an immense capital investment which has been provided by the community; the community should have such access to them as is compatible with their effective daytime use. (p. 46)

The report recommended that community schools should be developed in all areas but particularly in educational priority areas. Interestingly, one of its other recommendations was that two deputy headteachers might be assigned to each school with one being responsible for out-of-school activities – a very accurate recognition of the additional work which extended activities can place upon school staff.

From this promising start, community provision moved in fits and starts, dependent upon short-term funding, local and national initiatives and the aspirations of some individuals and the communities themselves. Funding always remained an issue, as the school budget could not be touched by extended provision.

With the Education Act 2002, governing bodies were at last allowed to provide a range of extended activities in and around the school with the DCSF's blessing. Schools were asked to consult with pupils, staff, parents and carers, local communities and the local authority to ensure the services to be developed were appropriate.

The Children Act 2004 took these promising indications a step further. It asked local authorities to work with key partners to strategically plan, commission and coordinate extended services. Closely on its heels, 'Extended Schools: Access to opportunities and services for all' (DfES, 2005) was published. This document, described as a prospectus, sets out the vision, timetable, funding and sources of practical support available. It recognizes that teachers are not in a position to take on all the additional responsibilities proposed and instead emphasizes the role that parents and the wider community should have. However, managing to muster all the component groups is no easy matter, as extended services coordinators have quickly discovered.

Here and now – what is an extended school?

There is no blueprint for an extended school. The intention is that all families have access to the 'core offer' through schools by 2010. This includes:

- high-quality 'wraparound' childcare provided (primary schools) on the school site or through other local providers, available 8 am to 6 pm all year round or to reflect community demand;
- a varied menu of activities to be on offer such as homework clubs and study support, sport, music tuition, special interest clubs and volunteering;
- parenting support including information sessions for parents at key transition points, parenting programmes and family learning sessions;
- swift and easy access to a wide range of specialist support services such as speech and language therapy, family support services and behaviour support;
- provision for wider community access to ICT, sports and arts facilities, including adult learning.

Not all schools in a locality will offer all these services. However, every family should be able to either access these facilities at their local school or be signposted (directed) to another accessible community building where they can.

Schools have started from too many different points for there to be a required path to extended status. Some schools had already developed many aspects of the core offer under their own steam. Others had been reluctant to dabble. And with good reason. Developing extended services takes time, effort and manpower. The very schools which can benefit most from extended services are often the ones which demand the most energy from their staff.

The patchwork of provision across the country is astounding as befits any innovation allowed to develop locally. Various permutations have appeared with numerous roles attached to them. Cluster coordinators, extended services development officers, community and learning partnership coordinators, consortium leaders and extended services coordinators are just some of the titles emerging. A vast array of new titles and job descriptions have appeared. Different combinations not just between authorities but within authorities too.

This book aims to provide advice, templates, pro formas and guidance recognizing that its audience is as diverse as the catchments they serve, the history they represent and the points they are starting from. Whatever your role, we hope that our signposting will help you with yours.

2 The extended services coordinator

Chapter aims

- To introduce the extended services coordinator role
- To identify the qualities needed in a coordinator
- To help you get to know your schools
- To help you establish systems for yourself

Topics

- Appointing a coordinator
- Introducing yourself
- Methods of communicating
- Keeping your head above water

Online resources

- 2.1 ESC job description
- 2.2 Collating information

Developing extended services in one school or across a cluster includes many challenges. You are engaged in a grand liaison activity between a vast number of services with varying policies, procedures and systems. Not everyone will be 'on board'. You will come across staff in all services who are sceptical about the principles of extended services. You will also come across those that profess to be supportive but who will show little enthusiasm for anything you are trying to establish. Some staff will make constant referrals and others would appear not to know that you exist.

There will be times when you will need to take time out and reflect on the real reasons that you wanted to be an extended services coordinator. You should to remind yourself that it is a vital role that brings together services in order to support the needs of children and their families, and that you can make a vast difference to the quality of life of those around you. This chapter considers some of the very special qualities that you will need as an extended services coordinator and how, once appointed, you might take the first steps in getting to know your schools.

Your appointment

Before making the appointment, the cluster of schools that appoint the extended services coordinator (ESC) should have discussed different aspects of the role. These will include:

- determining within the cluster who will be your line manager;
- identifying where different resources will come from – for example, a desk, laptop, mobile telephone and access to photocopying, stationery, etc.

The ESC has to be a very special person. Someone who can communicate with a broad range of people; someone who can empathize but also make tough decisions. Perhaps most importantly, the role may require a range of qualifications and experience that are very different from those normally attached to the school's existing staff. Experience in schools is not necessarily the driving factor. More important is that the ESC is able to build links within the community and work with parents and school staff. The route towards being an ESC might be a very unconventional one.

Key characteristics of an ESC might include:

- being able to work on own initiative and to feel their way through – to be a self-starter;

- having good time management skills (particularly if dividing time between schools);
- being willing to attend meetings, conferences, forums and networks;
- possessing good communication skills in order to consult with the relevant stakeholders throughout the schools and community;
- being able to adapt consultation methods and approaches as necessary (i.e. low levels of literacy);
- being able to prioritize and make decisions without constant supervision;
- having the ability to form partnerships with other agencies and to request their services;
- being motivated to go into the community to identify what is taking place, conducting research by contacting venues and collecting information;
- being willing to apply for funding and to monitor and evaluate any funding received;
- having organization skills to arrange cluster meetings, steering groups meetings, events, open days, etc;
- possessing good IT skills to produce questionnaires, posters, leaflets, reports, monitoring and evaluating documents.

The job description

The role is an exceedingly complex one which will vary enormously according to:

- the stage of development of extended provision in the school(s);
- the job descriptions of existing staff;
- the number of schools involved;
- the characteristics and needs of the community.

However, in most cases the ESC will be engaged in:

- liaising between providers (voluntary and private), services and schools;
- auditing and formulating a strategic plan;
- monitoring and evaluating this plan;

- supporting individual schools in developing their extended services provision;
- developing provision to meet the requirements of the core offer across the cluster;
- reporting back to the cluster group;
- training and development both as a trainee and a trainer.

For a more detailed breakdown of the ESC role see online resource 2.1 'ESC job description'. 2.1

Introducing yourself

You have been appointed, the celebrations are over and day one is fast approaching. Now you have to develop a systematic approach for familiarizing yourself with your schools and enabling them to get to know you. If you are working with a cluster of schools, unless you live geographically very close, you will need not only to get to know the schools themselves but also their communities. Use the following ten steps to help you in your first stages of picking up the reins.

Ten steps for getting to know your schools

1 Locate a map of the area and mark all the schools on it. It really helps to identify where they are situated geographically and to determine if you could signpost within the cluster. Not everyone will travel outside their immediate community.

2 Drive to each school to collect a prospectus. This will include plenty of useful information such as after-school activities, partner agencies, childcare, etc. In addition, you will now have a visual image of the school – putting a face to the name. It will continue to be a useful reference and you will need to request the updated version annually.

3 Whilst at the school, look at any community information boards and newsletters, picking up copies, if available. Keep this information ready for when you complete the audit.

4 Introduce yourself to any available members of staff. If you have just dropped in, it is unlikely that you will be able to meet with the headteacher and most members of teaching staff. If you haven't already met them previously, try to arrange a mutually convenient time when you can make your formal introductions and ensure that they have contact details and information.

5 In the meantime, continue with your research. Investigate the school's website and download any relevant information such as school profile, after-school activity timetable or newsletters. Download a copy of each school's recent Ofsted report, from Ofsted's website. This will highlight the school's strengths and any development areas that could be linked to the core offer (i.e., low levels of literacy could be improved through family learning).

6 Ask the schools for their catchment area and feeder schools. This will help you to become familiar with your schools' communities, particularly when signposting to activities. You need to take into consideration those parents/carers without transport to community venues. Determine the relevant children's centre and church, if relevant for each school, as schools will signpost towards these for activities and services.

7 Make a table to include the school names, addresses, head's name and telephone number. This can also be used to give to partners during meetings. Use the online resource 2.2 'Collating information' to help you.

2.2

8 Arrange to meet the headteacher of each school and any key members of staff, making a note of names and contacts as you go along. Work at forming a relationship with each headteacher in the cluster and key members of staff, such as the receptionist, caretaker and learning mentors. Check on the best methods of making contact and the times when they are most likely to be available.

9 Investigate the main community venues, apart from children's centres and churches, that you can signpost towards such as libraries, community centres, clubs for young people, leisure centres, residents' associations, community cafes and day centres.

10 Establish who you will need to work with on the school audit and arrange a time to meet with them to complete this (see Chapter 3).

Meeting the staff

The more staff you liaise with at your schools, the more people will understand your role. If you are able to, arrange to speak to all staff at a staff meeting. Introducing yourself in this way ensures that no one feels left out and that you don't hear months into your job 'Who is she/he anyway?' Make sure that staff know you can be approached directly if necessary. Be aware that some staff members will think that you are there to create extra work for them. You have to assure them that your work is grounded in the needs of the community and not to bolt-on activities for the sake of it.

Governing body

You might also want to consider attending a full governing body meeting as a guest. You could even be asked to be a school governor. Think carefully about this. Being a school governor is a time-consuming business. It requires your attendance in the evenings when it is already likely that some aspects of your role will also demand this. If you are a governor at one school and then turn down the opportunity at another, this might cause some ill-feeling. However, being a school governor certainly provides insight into the working of a school and will bring you closer to some members of the school community. Alternatively you might send an introductory letter or pack to the governing body explaining about your role.

The PTA or 'friends of'

Meeting the chair of the PTA is another way of introducing yourself to your school and finding out more about them. Depending on the make up of your PTA they represent another way into the community and will have their own ideas about how the school might extend its services. Again, you will need to consider the level to which you would want to be involved on a day-to-day basis and will need to be 'precious' about your allocation of time.

Attendance at PTA events can be a good way of meeting more people in an informal and relaxed environment. PTA fund raising can also be a means of subsidizing clubs and activities and purchasing specific resources that the school budget might not be able to fund.

The parents

Much of your role involves working with parents. The families of the pupils in your schools are a key component in the extended services agenda. You need to be approachable and show from the beginning that you work for them as well as the school. You need to establish as soon as you can the formal and informal ways of meeting your parents. These may include:

- having a profile in the playground – you have a captive audience just before the school bell;
- parents' evenings, open days, sports days – you can walk round, chat or set up a stall to highlight your role;
- setting up a drop-in session where parents can come and chat to you informally;
- arranging a coffee morning or other informal way of inviting parents in to meet you (see Chapter 9 for more information on engaging parents).

The pupils

Your direct involvement with pupils will be constrained by time. However, pupils should be aware of who you are and feel able to talk to you about their school and their needs. It is worthwhile ensuring that they know about your role through:

- meeting them in assembly and introducing yourself;
- attending a school council session and consulting with them about school provision;
- introducing yourself through the school newsletter (this informs parents as well);
- spending some time at break and lunchtime in the playground chatting with the pupils and joining in games if you can;
- taking part in the occasional school trip or club to keep yourself informed about the pupils and their likes and dislikes.

Involving yourself in the occasional school trip, particularly when staff are struggling to find the personnel, will be very much appreciated.

Methods of communicating

You cannot be in all schools at once. Therefore, establishing your diary, finding ways of sharing it and ensuring that you can be reached even when you are not immediately accessible is particularly important. You may find it difficult sometimes to draw yourself away from the school that hosts you. The emerging issues or problems in that school will be particularly real to you and will sometimes demand your attention when you have an appointment elsewhere.

Be careful. Others schools in the cluster will soon pick up on the signals if they feel they are being neglected. You may need to work hard to ensure your time is not monopolized by any particular school and maintain the commitments you have. Of course, if there is a real emergency, all your schools will understand the need to change the schedule – just make sure they are informed and are aware of the reason why. Misunderstandings most often occur when communication is insufficient.

Not all your schools will be as engaged with the extended services agenda. You will need to continue to encourage your less enthusiastic schools and keep them informed of what is going on. This might include sending them newsletters, bulletins and other ideas and updates to hopefully tempt them in.

You need to know the best way of communicating with each school. Who will be your main contact? You will need to establish:

- who you ring in an emergency;
- who you should email with bulletins and updates;
- who will attend the cluster meetings;
- where you should send information;
- how to contact the headteachers when you need to speak to them.

Emailing

Confirm the email address that should be used to communicate with the headteacher and office staff. Some headteachers use a Yahoo or Hotmail email address while some use the school's general administration email address. Email is often a good way to contact schools as it is not determined by lesson times and assemblies. It is a particularly useful method for sending out bulletins to all your schools. With a minimum of effort they are reminded of your presence and kept in the loop.

Coordinators are often bombarded with emails and phone calls from providers, especially after-school providers. Be selective on sending this information to schools. You could save this for the cluster meeting or collate them into one document, such as a newsletter.

Visits

The audit can be completed once a year, but in the interim you will visit schools depending on the development areas that arise and if they wish you to attend events, etc. You will probably find that you will visit some schools more than others – this is normal. It depends on schools' understanding of your role and the work that you can do to assist them.

Written communication

Creating a newsletter to the headteachers is a good way of keeping them informed of your progress and to update on local schemes, providers, courses, parenting training, etc.

Report back to schools on progress by completing monthly reports, action plans, PowerPoint presentations or utilizing project management tools. This will help to show progress.

Meetings

Organize a cluster meeting for once a term to update on progress, share information and discuss problems. This meeting can also be used to direct the cluster and agree priorities. Depending on the makeup of the schools in the cluster, the forward focus may not be a joint consensus, as some schools will prefer to have individual development work with their school. Use general themes, such as family learning, adult learning or parenting support, to direct the cluster focus and attempt to agree cluster priorities for the forthcoming year.

Keeping your head above water

Depending on how many schools you have responsibility for, there can be an issue with ensuring that you are there for everyone and yet are able to add real value. Don't try to spread yourself too thinly! Instead try the following:

- Liaise with other local cluster coordinators or those in a community focused role. You will be able to share contacts and best practice, which can save time.
- Work with other local coordinators in a geographical area and take it in turns to attend meetings, networks and forums.
- Work together with other coordinators to produce holiday leaflets, parent newsletters or signposting information.
- If working for a cluster of schools, produce the newsletter or holiday activity leaflet and email to schools for them to copy and distribute themselves.
- Email information to schools – it is easier than navigating around lesson times, assemblies and meetings.
- When making new contacts, determine whether it is really necessary to meet them. If they are a provider visiting all local coordinators, then have them come to a cluster coordinator meeting.
- Participate in sharing best practice with other coordinators and they may do the same, which will save you time.

- Create a website to promote extended services activities and have links to other local activities and services. Holiday activity leaflets and newsletters could be promoted here, rather than photocopying.
- Collate new information for schools and present in the newsletter to headteachers or at a meeting.

3 Starting point – the audit

Chapter aims

- To help you identify what provision might be included in the core offer
- To help you identify where your school/cluster is in terms of extended services provision
- To help you identify what your next priorities should be in relation to individual schools and the cluster as a whole

Topics

- Tips for auditing provision
- What the core offer might look like
- Auditing schools and cluster mapping
- Establishing your priorities

Figures

Tables

Online resources

- 3.1 What the core offer could look like
- 3.2 Extended services audit form – template
- 3.3 School development areas form – template
- 3.4 Auditing across a cluster form – worked example
- 3.4a Auditing across a cluster form – template
- 3.5 Cluster development areas form – template

Whatever aspect of provision you are looking to develop, it is worth starting with an audit. You cannot really know what needs to be done until you have checked what is already out there. There is nothing more frustrating than to spend days developing provision only to discover it's already being done by someone else.

Tips for auditing provision

You're new to the role. Perhaps just appointed. You've got lots of ideas and enthusiasm abounds. Perhaps you're responsible for ten schools, perhaps for just one. Where do you start?

It can be tempting to rush straight in and start implementing everything you promised at interview. Or perhaps you are anxious to please and keen to put into practice every idea suggested by your colleagues. In one word – STOP. The worst mistake you can make is to begin rushing headlong down a path before checking whether it's going in the right direction.

There will be some people in your school who have been waiting for a long time to be able to 'delegate' a favourite hobby horse. Until you have had time to settle in and take stock, it is dangerous to start anything. There are exceptions. If you are replacing someone previously appointed, you will have a different challenge to face. You will still need to audit but may find that there are projects that are desperately in need of maintenance or are in need of resuscitation. In these cases, your energy now could save time later.

So, the general rule is to audit first. If anyone should ask you about any pet project they would like established, make a note of their ideas, ask them for some details about it and explain the stage you are at and that when you have assessed what's currently on offer, you will come back to them.

Top tips for auditing

- 3.2 Completing the school audits can be time consuming, but they are a good way of familiarizing yourself with the school. Use online resource 3.2 'Extended services audit form' to help you to focus on the required information and build a picture of what the school offers.
- Complete the audit once a year, even if the schools are core compliant. These are a good talking point and can help to focus on the core offer.
- It is advisable to complete the audit form yourself as schools may have different interpretations of the core offer.
- Find out when the school last consulted its local community and parents and ask for copies. If the school has a consultation process already in place, it will save time. If they do not consult regularly, ask if you can, or do a joint effort with the school.
- During the audit, ask about key staff members such as the school nurse, learning mentors and family support workers. These members of staff will be aware of the agencies that are working in the school.
- Schools may not always know the difference between family learning and parenting programmes. Be prepared to explain this one.
- During development discussions, ask schools if they have a wish list of activities or services they would like to offer. Always ask about funding, where the evidence of need is captured and how the activity will be sustainable.
- Find out how the school currently signposts to the areas of the core offer that are not provided on site. You could perhaps help with this. Think about websites, noticeboards and newsletters.
- 3.4 Compile each school's audit information across the cluster (see online resource 3.4 'Auditing across a cluster form') – it will help to maintain an overall picture of provision.
- 3.4 & 3.4a Always keep an eye on the local press. If you have a large number of schools, you cannot be there every day and newspaper articles can help keep you informed. New initiatives are launched constantly and this information will provide currency for your 'Auditing across a cluster' map (see online resources 3.4 and 3.4a).
- Always make a distinction between what is delivered by the school and what is delivered by external providers. Ask for names of these providers – these are great contacts that you could share between your schools.

What the core offer could look like

> By 2010 all children should have access to a range of extended services in and around their school. (TDA website)

So what is the core offer (Table 3.1)?

Table 3.1 Core offer summary

School	**Core offer**
Primary schools	High-quality *childcare* 8 am to 6 pm, five days a week, 48 weeks a year – combined with a varied menu of activities
Secondary schools	Varied menu of *study support* and enrichment activities
All schools	Access to *parenting support* and *parenting programmes* *Signposting* to national and local sources of information, advice and support through *family learning* sessions
All schools – particularly early years	*Integrated working* with other services – identification of children with additional needs as early as possible
All schools	*Community access* to appropriate facilities Access to *adult learning*

A core offer summary table is also provided in online resource 3.1 'What the core offer could look like'. 3.1

Usually, it is not appropriate for all schools to provide all the core offer. The key is for a cluster or local area to ensure that there is access to all facilities within that area. Duplication is to be avoided almost as much as omission. With a limited amount of resources, it is vital that what is available is channelled appropriately. This is where the extended services coordinator is vital. It is about ensuring that as many of the potential services can be provided as the community needs. And this will differ.

3.4a

The following are examples of the different provision that might be offered under each core offer (for more examples see online resource 3.4a 'Auditing across a cluster form').

Core offer 1

Primary schools provide access to high-quality childcare, 8 am to 6pm, five days a week, 48 weeks a year, in accordance with their communities' needs, combined with a varied menu of activities (study support) to enhance achievement and broaden interests

For example:

- breakfast clubs
- after-school clubs
- holiday clubs
- pre-school facilities
- crèches
- sports clubs
- study support
- arts and crafts workshops
- dance and drama clubs
- ICT clubs
- gifted and talented programmes
- music tuition
- cookery
- activities weeks
- self-esteem programmes
- inter-school competitions
- intergenerational activities

Core offer 2

Secondary schools provide access to a varied menu of study support and enrichment activities which provide fun and stimulating activities for young people, as well as a safe place to be

For example:

- homework clubs
- study support
- sports clubs
- chess clubs
- music tuition
- foreign languages
- dance and drama
- arts and crafts
- volunteering opportunities
- enterprise education
- 'catch up' or 'stretch' activities
- gifted and talented programmes
- holiday clubs
- youth offer
- advice on drugs and health issues
- school sport partnerships
- sports leaders
- Duke of Edinburgh Award
- computer games club
- self-esteem programmes
- inter-school competitions
- intergenerational activities
- babysitting courses

Core offer 3

Schools provide access to parenting support, including information sessions for parents of pupils joining reception and on transfer to secondary school; signposting to national and local sources of information, advice and support; access to parenting groups using structured, evidence-based parenting programmes; and family learning sessions to allow children to learn with their parents, where consultation has shown there is a demand

For example:

- new parents evening
- transition evenings
- family information service
- school newsletters
- share programme
- behaviour management information
- keeping up with the children
- dads and lads
- PTA events (fetes, barbecues, bingo, barn dances)
- parents' coffee morning
- reading in class
- volunteering in school
- school nurse drop-in
- parents evening
- family literacy and numeracy programmes
- translation services
- toy libraries
- parents' forum
- parent governors
- internet safety sessions

Core offer 4

Swift and easy access: working closely with other statutory services and the voluntary and community sector, schools ensure that children with additional needs are identified as early as possible, and are well supported through integrated working with other services

For example:

- speech and language therapy
- child and adolescent mental health services
- family support services
- intensive behaviour support
- sexual health services
- counselling services
- drug and alcohol services
- teenage pregnancy services
- domestic violence teams
- local police
- relate
- bereavement services
- special educational needs support services
- educational social worker services
- connexions
- social services
- educational psychologists
- therapeutic services
- drop-in health sessions
- credit unions

For more detailed information about the services mentioned above, see Chapter 5.

Core offer 5

Schools ensure they provide community access to appropriate facilities, such as ICT suites, sports and arts facilities, and also provide access to adult learning

For example:

- ICT clubs (including email, internet, digital photography)
- sports
- arts
- community and voluntary groups
- martial arts groups
- first aid courses
- nutritional awareness courses
- managing finances courses
- job hunting (interviews and CVs) guidance
- adult learners' weeks
- local colleges and training providers
- fitness/ aerobics classes
- language courses
- recycling programmes
- book clubs
- life skills courses
- intergenerational activities
- ESOL
- adult and community learning

Auditing schools and cluster mapping

You now need to know what each school in your cluster is providing. One difficulty is ensuring that everything is covered but not duplicated. A major task for the ESC is ensuring that within the cluster a wide range of facilities and services are provided. This is complicated by the fact that schools have been developing their own provision over years. This will have taken them in their own unique directions. You need to find out what they have in place and what they'd like to provide. In order to do that you need to do the following:

3.2

- Step 1 – complete the 'Extended services audit form' for your schools (online resource 3.2) ideally during a meeting with your link person.

3.3

- Step 2 – complete the 'School development areas form' for your schools (online resource 3.3) in order to establish what schools would like to develop next.

3.4a

- Step 3 – bring the audit information together on the 'Auditing across a cluster' form (online resource 3.4a). This should highlight where there are any gaps in provision.

Step 1

3.2

You should arrange to meet with a representative from each school to complete the 'Extended services audit' form. (A worked example is given in Figure 3.1 and a template is provided in online resource 3.2.) You could leave this with schools for completion but may find that there will be differences in the way that each one completes it and that interpretation of the core offer can vary. In order to ensure consistency, it is beneficial for you to ask directly about the core offer and to explore the aspects of provision that schools may have neglected to mention.

This personal link with key people at each school is vital. Unless you are based solely in one school you will be reliant upon school personnel for implementation. The relationship you develop with them is essential.

Extended services audit

Date	
School Information	
School name:	St James Infant School
Headteacher:	John Smith
Contact name (if different to head):	Carol Jones
Pupils on roll:	246
Learning mentor/family support worker/parent support advisor:	Laura Thomas
School nurse name:	Sarah Bagley
Designated person for child protection:	John Smith
Consultation Information	
Date of last consultation:	September 2009
School council contact:	Liz Waine
Date of next parents' evening:	June (Year 3 Induction)
Core Offer Information	
Childcare: • Breakfast club • After-school club • Holiday • Wrap-around care • Pre-school • Nursery	List clubs and providers: Breakfast club and after-school run by local provider on site Links with local childminders

Varied menu of activities: • Before-school clubs • Lunchtime clubs • After-school clubs • Holiday clubs • Study support	List activities and providers: *Breakfast club: Go Sports (Mon & Wed)* *After school: dance, football and netball (school delivered)* *Holiday: Playscheme (Leisure Trust)* *Produces leaflets to signpost for holidays*
Parent support: • Newsletters • Workshops • Link books • PTA/'Friends of…' groups • Parents' evenings • Group calling/text • Transition sessions	List activities and providers: *Half-termly newsletter* *PTA* *Parents' workshops* *Community noticeboard* *Transition sessions*
Parenting programmes: • Handling teenage behaviour • Working with fathers • What to tell the children about relationships and sex • Triple P	List activities and providers: *Triple P*
Community access: • Community lettings • School holiday lettings • Adult learning lettings • Community and voluntary groups • Informal meetings • Free community access	List activities and group names: *Local netball team use school* *Slimming World hire hall* *Muslim weddings* *Locality meetings in hall*

Adult learning: • School-delivered provision • Adult and community learning • Local FE college provision • Community and voluntary organizations	List activities and providers: *Local FE college deliver adult learning opportunities* *School delivers adult literacy classes*
Family learning: • Keeping up with the children • Storysacks • Cookery • IT courses • Internet safety	List activities and providers: *Local council's adult learning provision offers 'keeping up with the children'* *School has run internet safety sessions*
Swift and Easy Access to Agencies linked to the school: • Speech and language • Counselling • Education social work • Benefits/advice • Debt counselling • Primary Care Trust • Teenage pregnancy • Youth agencies • Community and voluntary groups	List activities and providers: *Elm Counselling Service* *Family information services* *Citizens Advice Bureau* *Education psychologist* *Relate*
Form completed by:	

Note: the examples given for each area of the core offer are not exhaustive. They are there to serve as prompts.

Figure 3.1 Extended services audit form – worked example

Step 2

During your meeting you should take the opportunity to discuss with schools what they would like to do next. Your conversation might include:

- the projects they are already considering;
- any relevant objectives included on their school development plan;
- any other opportunities/information they think might be useful to share;
- any possible funding they may be able to access.

Figure 3.2 is a worked example of the plans that an individual school might
3.3 have (a template of this form is provided in online resource 3.3).

School development areas – Summer 2009				
School 1:				
List developments against core offer area below.				
Core offer	**School priorities for development and evidence of need/ partners**	**Costings/ timescales**	**Actions**	**Success criteria**
Childcare	Have surveyed parents – results show insufficient demand currently			
Varied menu of activities	School would like to offer more after-school activities. School does not have appropriate staff. School would like providers to come in and offer different activities, i.e. science, art and crafts, cheerleading, singing	School will not charge provider to use the premises. The provider can charge the children	ESC to inform possible clubs Clubs to contact link person at school	At least two additional clubs are established
Parent support	Not currently a development priority			
Parenting programmes	School would like to offer parenting courses in-house. The school has a teaching assistant who is interested in delivering parenting courses. School will release the teaching assistant to go on training	Cost of training	ESC to identify potential courses	Course is established for summer term 2009

Core offer	School priorities for development and evidence of need/ partners	Costings/ timescales	Actions	Success criteria
Community access	School is interested in encouraging more community groups to use the facilities. School has a lettings policy	School will charge £25.00 per hour	ESC to discuss possibilities with school bursar	At least one additional community group is using the premises
Adult learning	No plans in place			
Family learning	No plans in place			
Swift and easy access to agencies	No plans in place			

Figure 3.2 School development areas form – worked example

Step 3

You should now have extensive information about what is currently available and what your individual schools would like to accomplish. There might be some omissions. The member of staff you met with may not be aware of everything that is happening. For the time being you will have to accept this until you become more familiar with your schools.

Be prepared for schools getting in touch with you throughout the year to communicate changing development priorities. For example after:

- data analysis (RAISEonline)
- completion of the SEF (Self-Evaluation Form)
- setting of the new school budget
- evaluation of the SIDP (Single-Integrated Development Plan).

These updates will require you to amend your own individual school development priorities.

You need to collate all the information from your schools in order to produce an across-cluster view. Using the online resource form 'Auditing across a cluster' (3.4 worked example and 3.4a template) to help you, map out the provision across your schools against the core offer. 3.4 & 3.4a

Establishing your priorities

3.4 & 3.4a

Now you have your map in front of you (online resources 3.4 and 3.4a) that details what schools currently offer and their individual priorities. What happens next? You need to establish a cluster-based strategy as well as keep a high profile on the individual plans that schools have. In order to do that you need:

- Step 1 – look across each core offer from the 'Auditing across a cluster' form (online resources 3.4 and 3.4a) and note any aspects of provision that you think are missing.

3.5

- Step 2 – complete the 'Cluster development areas' form (Figure 3.3, online resource 3.5) including the priorities for individual schools
- Step 3 – negotiate the developments across the cluster and complete the 'Actions/ success criteria', 'To be completed by/when' and 'Funding from...' section of the 'Cluster development areas' form (online resource 3.5) where you are able to.

Step 1

Table 3.2 provides an example of one core offer and the types of provision already in existence at three of your schools.

Table 3.2 Identifying gaps in the cluster

Identifying gaps in the cluster	
Schools provide access to parenting support, including information sessions for parents of pupils joining reception and on transfer to secondary school; signposting to national and local sources of information, advice and support; access to parenting groups	
Primary school 1	Curriculum workshops, half-termly newsletter, link books, school nurse sessions, family learning, parents' evening, PTA
Primary school 2	Parents' evening, PTA, community noticeboard, parent coffee mornings, parenting programme
Primary school 3	Parents' evening, PTA, parents' forum
Secondary school	Transition evenings, family literacy and numeracy, school nurse drop-in, bilingual book exchange

Looking at these schools and what they provide against core offer 3, you might identify the following omissions:

- Opportunities for parents volunteering and helping in school.
- Opportunities for parents to find out more about how to help their children.
- Targeted support for parents facing particular issues.

You will then need to complete a 'Cluster development areas' form (online resource 3.5, also see Figure 3.3) in order to have an overview of what is needed within the cluster. 3.5

Be aware that some omissions may be filled by other local and community provision. Just because it doesn't exist within your cluster of schools doesn't mean that it is not available. Meeting with other community providers is necessary in order to help with this. For example:

- children's centres
- local voluntary groups
- religious groups within the community
- childminding network
- private childcare providers.

More information about this is provided in Chapter 4.

Step 2

Now complete the 'Cluster development areas' form (online resource 3.5, see Figure 3.3) 'Current omissions' row. This will help you build up a picture of what is needed. At this stage it is also important to keep in mind the development priorities for individual schools. Are there any schools that have similar requests or priorities where you can combine resources? Do include individual school's priorities on this pro forma as you will not have time to refer back to all the individual 'School development areas'. It is important that you combine them altogether into one single plan. 3.5

Cluster development areas				
Completed following analysis of the 'Extended services audit' and 'School development areas'				
Core offer	**Cluster development priority** **Individual school priority**	**Actions/success criteria**	**To be completed by/ when**	**Funded by…***
Childcare	There is insufficient after-school care between the schools. There is no childcare for working parents	Contact LA for advice on possible providers Survey parents to check on feasibility of school 3 hosting	Every Child Matters (ECM) autumn 2009 ECM summer term 2009	Start-up funding
	School 3 is interested in the possibility of hosting an outside provider	Working parents have access to after-school childcare		

Varied menu of activities	A broader range of alternative provision is needed	Make links between external providers and schools Introduce external providers to learning mentor at school 1	ECM summer 2009 ECM summer 2009	Support available from PTA
	School 1 would like a more varied menu of activities provided by external providers	At least three new clubs established broadening the range of activities available to pupils		
Parent support	Need for targeted support for parents including – relate, counselling, advice on housing opportunities for parents volunteering in schools	ECM to speak to school counselling service Learning mentor to leaflet parents about counselling service	ECM summer 2009 Learning mentor summer 2009	Free service to schools
	School 3 would like to provide a counselling service for families	Counselling service to be established supporting families in need		
Core offer	Cluster development priorities	Actions/success criteria	To be completed by/when	Funded by…
	Individual school priority			

Parenting programmes	Opportunities for parents to find out how to help their children	ECM makes links with 'Keeping up with the children' providers ECM to locate training opportunities for TAs TAs to be released and courses organized	ECM summer term 2009 ECM summer term 2009 School leadership team autumn 2009	School budget subsidized course
	School 1 would like to offer parenting courses in-house	TAs receive training and are able to run courses in the autumn term providing support to parents		
Community access	Local clubs tend to use the secondary school – need to consider spreading use	Provide guidance for school 1's bursar on increasing number of lettings	ECM to meet with school 1's bursar – summer term 2009	Continued funding of bursar role
	School 1 would like to increase its number of lettings	School 1 doubles number of community lettings		
Adult learning	Need for programmes to support parents in accessing work opportunities	Link school 4's business manager with adult learning course coordinator for LA	Business manager to meet with adult learning coordinator – summer term 2009 Club to run autumn term 2009	Partnership working funding
	School 4 has expressed interest in preparation for work courses	Course established and at least 16 adults improving their chances of finding employment		

Family learning	Need to increase number of family learning opportunities	School 1 invites art coordinators from schools 2 and 3 to see art class	Art coordinator school 1 summer term 2009	School art budget
	Good practice in school 1 with family art classes – encourage other schools to share	Family art class runs in at least one other school – extending family learning opportunities		
Swift and easy access to agencies	High profile of school nurse – lack of involvement from other agencies	ECM to arrange link with bereavement counselling service	ECM summer term 2009	Local authority budget
	School 3 request for bereavement counselling	Counselling service provides advice to school 3 on bereavement – family supported		
Current omissions				

*More information on funding can be found in Chapter 8.

Figure 3.3 Cluster development areas – worked example

Step 3

Negotiate the developments across the cluster and complete the 'Actions/success criteria', 'To be completed by/ when' 'Funded by...' sections of the 'Cluster development areas' pro forma where you are able to.

You will need to balance the needs of individual schools and the cluster. Somehow you need to bring these together and it won't always be easy. For example, you might find that a school has a particular interest in providing childcare after school. Perhaps they think it might attract parents to the school. However, it might be in the best interest of the cluster for provision to be more central and at a venue where collections might be made from other schools.

In the end, schools and their governing bodies can decide what they would like to offer. You can only proffer advice and steer in the direction you feel is most beneficial. Perhaps there is some other resource or activity that they might be encouraged to take on instead? They may also recognize the difficulties involved in making the childcare financially accessible if insufficient children can be attracted from neighbouring schools.

Be prepared for changes. This planning is a guide that will help you see the micro and macro within your role. However, you will often feel thwarted by changing members of staff, school politics and the external pressures on schools, which will sometimes result in unavoidable changes for you. Smile!

4 Consulting your community

Chapter aims

- To help you establish who is in your community
- To help you develop a dialogue with members of the community
- To provide ideas for consulting the community
- To help you develop community cohesion
- To help you audit against the duty to promote community cohesion

Topics

- Who is in your community?
- Finding out what they think
- Developing community cohesion

Figures

Tables

Online resources

The term 'community' is not easily translated into one group of people. Our understanding of it will vary according to how wide we want to draw the circle and how we distinguish between groups.

The Ofsted document 'Inspecting maintained schools' duty to promote community cohesion: guidance for inspectors' (Ofsted 2010) identifies the following levels in relation to the school's community:

1. The immediate community within the school.
2. The community where the schools are situated.
3. The UK community.
4. The global community.

For the extended services coordinator, 'community' is likely to reflect the local picture. It might include:

- all those attending the school either for work or as a student;
- religious groups within the immediate environment of the school;
- ethnic minority groups within the immediate community;
- different socio-economic groups within the community;
- local clubs, societies and groups that meet together locally with particular interests;
- local businesses and places of work;
- families with similar medical/learning needs.

Who is in your community?

This is not a simple question to answer and you will need to speak with a range of people in order to establish what their perceptions of the school community are. They will differ. Piecing together the range of people who could be classed as part of the community will take time but it is worth persevering. The groups might include the following.

Parents, pupils and staff

You will have already collected information about school roll, numbers, contacts etc. as part of your audit. Ideally you have also:

- spoken with the chair of the PTA
- spoken with the chair of the governing body
- introduced yourself in assembly to the pupils
- met the staff at a staff meeting
- introduced yourself to parents either through a newsletter, by spending time in the playground or as part of a drop-in.

However, if you are responsible for a large number of schools you will not have time to do all this for each school. If this is the case, you may need to find some shortcuts to making introductions which could include as a minimum:

- an introduction on a school newsletter
- a stall at a parents' evening
- a five minute slot at a staff meeting.

It might be easier for you to engage in more introductory activities at your host school. This can still provide you with insight into the local community generally, particularly if you can spend some time talking to the governing body and PTA. If based in the local secondary school, some of the parents you meet may well have pupils at local primary schools. You can use any opportunities you have to meet with them to ask them about local provision.

Religious groups

Figure 4.1 provides a format for recording details about local religious groups (available as online resource 4.1). Ideally you should meet with the religious leader and visit the place of worship. You will need to ask them: 4.1

- about their views of your schools;
- what they consider to be the major issues facing the local community;
- about the current links they have with local schools;
- about any possible links that might be developed.

Religious groups	
Religion:	Place of worship:
Name of religious leader:	Contact details:
Other details:	
Religion:	Place of worship:
Name of religious leader:	Contact details:
Other details:	
Religion:	Place of worship:
Name of religious leader:	Contact details:
Other details:	

Figure 4.1 Religious groups form

Ethnic minority groups

These groups can sometimes be quite difficult to meet and consult with. Language can be a significant barrier. Your best opportunity is to meet with any members of staff in the school, PTA or governing body who are members of these groups and/or act as links and identify with them the particular concerns and needs of the community. You might want to use Figure 4.2 to record some of the characteristics of the group (available as online resource 4.2). If you have time, try to make links with any local clubs and societies representing their specific interests. 4.2

Group 1	
Country of origin/region:	Main language spoken:
Main religion:	Groups and societies:
Other details:	

Figure 4.2 Ethnic minority groups audit

Do try to find out some of the background to any groups settling in the local area. Who are the main employers? What are the groups' views of the school? What issues arise in relation to the local schools? This might include:

- uniform
- language barriers
- term-time holidays and religious observance
- different expectations
- living circumstances

- perceptions of school staff
- financial difficulties
- understanding of school procedures.

Although some of these are related more to the religious needs of the community, the cultural and religious can be difficult to separate.

Different socio-economic groups

Different sections of your community will have very different needs depending upon their employment status and level of qualification. Depending upon your catchment there may be groups of hard-to-reach parents who have experienced difficulty in school and are reluctant to engage. These are some of the groups who need your input most. The challenge for the ESC is to find ways of reaching these groups and encouraging them to access the support they need.

You may find, initially, that you need to develop ways of meeting groups of parents outside the school building. Children's centres might be a good point of access as some of these parents will be more willing to engage with services during the child's early years.

Use the experience and knowledge of other professionals in the community. Your school nurse can be particularly beneficial as a means of finding out more about some of the neediest families, how they might be accessed and what they need. The educational social worker, if based locally for some time, will have in-depth knowledge about some of the requirements of hard-to-reach groups and individual families in particular. If these people are kept informed of what is available within the cluster, they will help encourage families to use the facilities and support available.

Don't be put off if you seem to make very little progress in encouraging some families to participate. There may be generations in a family who feel ostracized by local institutions and schools in particular. That will not be reversed in a few weeks. The most you can hope is to gradually open up a dialogue and enable some uptake of what is available.

More information about working with different groups of parents is included in Chapter 9.

Local clubs and societies

There will be many of these and you cannot be expected to know about all of them. However, you will want to gather as much knowledge as possible in order to know what's on offer for families and who might benefit. This subject is covered in more detail in Chapter 5.

Local businesses and places of work

Knowledge about local employers can be particularly beneficial when you are looking for sponsors and support for curriculum initiatives. Again, it is likely that those working in and around the school will already have collected this local knowledge. For example, Table 4.1 shows who you might ask.

Table 4.1 Who to ask about local employers

Who	**What they might know**
Chair of PTA	Shops, local businesses which are prepared to donate
Chair of governing body	Local businesses which have supported the governing body in the past. There may still be a co-opted member of the local business community on the governing body
Administrative staff	Local businesses that have made donations at different times for 'in kind' materials
Headteacher and senior leadership team	Members of the local business community who have perhaps: • sponsored school teams • contributed to assemblies • contributed to curriculum weeks • family in the school

It is important that local businesses feel that their involvement with the school is reciprocated. You need to consider what is in it for them when they become involved with the school on a project. Drawing attention to their support through publicity is one specific way in which you can pay them back for their involvement. You might also want to consider:

- inviting them to school events;
- linking individuals to a class;
- enabling pupils to go and visit them – for example, to sing carols at Christmas;
- pupils writing thank you cards or finding other ways of demonstrating; appreciation for their involvement.

Families with similar medical/learning needs

Some groups of pupils and their families may have a bond that comes from their particular type of need, such as families with dyslexic or autistic children or those with visual or hearing impairments. Charitable organizations exist which aim to support these groups of pupils and it is worth incorporating them in your plans. Consider what the specific needs of these groups might be within the extended school provision offered.

You might wish to facilitate targeted provision if there is a sufficient number with a particular need within your cohort of schools. You would need specialist help with this but organizations are generally supportive in your efforts. However, you should also be cautious as not all families will wish to be identified according to their need.

It is important to keep in mind that you must make accessibility for a full range of pupils and their families a priority. You will need to monitor the provision you establish for take-up by all groups. Ofsted expects that consideration is given to ensuring that extra-curricular activities are made available to all and that where a group is under-represented, every effort is made to redress the balance.

Finding out what they think

It is beneficial to ensure that you consult the stakeholders of your schools. However, with more than one school it can be very difficult to do so in any depth. To cut down on your work, using consultations and forums already established by your schools or local authorities can help. You might be able to add some targeted questions to an annual survey that they already distribute or attend a meeting of stakeholders where you can ask a small selection of questions of your own. Formal examples of how you have consulted are important. However, anecdotal information and comment can be valuable too.

Make sure you record clearly where you have surveyed and what the responses were. Note any particular actions you've been able to implement and what the outcomes of these have been. This will also be useful evidence for an Ofsted inspection, and for your own records, of course.

Surveys

Surveys can be a useful way of gathering evidence from a large number of people. An annual survey can enable a focus on an area for development and support the evaluation cycle. An example of a questionnaire for parents on the kind of support they would like can be found in online resource 4.3 'Parent or carer support questionnaire'. Surveys can be used on all sections of the community; however, the following points should be taken into consideration: 4.3

- It can be difficult to establish a meaningful survey for use with very young pupils. However, drawing how you feel can be a useful way of involving even the youngest.
- You will need to establish a balance between multiple-choice questions which are easier to analyse and open-ended questioning which can provide more insight but is difficult to summarize.
- Make sure that those you survey receive feedback on what they said and what actions will be taken as a result.
- Keep your questions simple and focused. Be sure about what you want to find out and stick to it.

- Consider providing additional support for ycunger pupils and those with special needs.
- Depending upon how you distribute them, there can be a low level of response.
- Make translated versions available so that all community members can access.
- Remember to provide feedback (an example is given in online resource 4.4 'Parent support questionnaire feedback'). 4.4

4.5 Figure 4.3 includes examples of some questions relating to community cohesion that might be given to members of school staff (available as online resource 4.5).

	Strongly agree	**Agree**	**Disagree**	**Strongly disagree**
I think this school works well with its community				
I think all groups are made welcome at our school				
I understand the needs of different groups at our school				
I am aware of any differences in the progress made by different groups				
I take actions to address any differences in rate of progress				
The curriculum reflects the different groups in our school				
The curriculum reflects the different groups in society				
I think our school includes an international perspective				
I think we use our local area well to help with teaching and learning				

Figure 4.3 Sample questions for staff on community cohesion

Figure 4.4 includes examples of some questions relating to community cohesion that might be given to parents (available as online resource 4.6).

4.6

	Strongly agree	Agree	Disagree	Strongly disagree
I think this school works well with its community				
I always feel welcome at the school				
I feel the staff understand my child's needs				
I feel that staff check on my child's progress regularly				
I feel that staff provide good guidance for my child to help him/her progress				
I think the curriculum my child studies is relevant to living in the twenty-first century				
My child learns about the different cultures and beliefs of people in our community				
My child learns about the different cultures and beliefs of people across the world				
My child is taught about the local area and the people living here				

Figure 4.4 Sample questions for parents on community cohesion

Forums

Your schools will have developed their own methods of collating information from their stakeholders. One of these might include a parents' forum – a group of parents who provide advice, ideas and guidance on a regular basis. If this is the case, you might find that you are able to attend one of these meetings or present a question for discussion as part of the agenda.

However, you should keep in mind that sometimes your role is particularly beneficial as you are not actually a member of school staff. There is value in you consulting independently from the school. Parents may share views with you that they will not share in a school-organized forum.

Interviews

This could either be a group interview or interviews of individuals. A group interview can be more relaxing for pupils and parents who may be rather intimidated by an individual interview. However, group interviews are vulnerable to the impact of one individual who dominates the group. They can also lead to copycat answers.

Interviews can be useful as they enable you to target particular groups who may need additional support or who may be under-represented in school activities generally. Be careful about asking permission for interviews of pupils and check with the school what procedure they would like you to follow.

Individual children can be selected across the school according to gender, ethnicity, religion, level of ability and social need. During any interview you will need to consider whether you make notes or record responses.

Both group and individual interviews are very time-consuming and so you cannot be expected to carry them out frequently and certainly not in all your schools. Be selective. If you have noticed there is a particular issue in one school with a group, target them specifically.

Meetings

Meetings already organized by the school can be good opportunities for you to consult with stakeholders. For example, you might attend a parents evening and survey parents waiting to see their child's class teacher. Attending a governors' meeting will provide you with the opportunity to ask questions of a cross-selection of adults associated with the school. Attending a PTA meeting is another opportunity to meet with members of the school community and ask them for their views.

Informal methods of 'finding out'

Through every encounter, walk and chat you will be finding out what people feel about your schools and what they offer. Walking around the playground at breaktimes and whilst parents are waiting to pick up their children can be particularly beneficial for catching the mood of pupils and parents.

If you have time, an informal coffee morning will allow parents to chat in a relaxed environment. This may encourage some of your parents who don't normally participate in the usual round of meetings.

School council

Most schools now have a school council. This is usually a representative group of students who meet regularly to discuss issues according to an agenda that is at least partly set by students at the school. They are usually elected by their peers and are a mixture of age groups. This can be a very good forum for the ESC to visit in order to discuss issues within his/her role. However, be cautious. Not all school councils are truly representative and you may need to find additional routes for ensuring that you hear views from across all groups in your schools.

There will usually be a member of staff within the school who has responsibility for the group and to whom you should take your request to visit. You should go prepared with a list of focused questions. For example:

- What clubs do you take part in?
- What do you think of these clubs?
- What clubs would you like to see running in the school?

When asking groups of pupils about their views and 'wishes', do make sure that they are aware that not everything is always possible. If they do make unrealistic suggestions, you must explain the reason why this may not be achievable.

Developing community cohesion

The official definition of community cohesion from DCSF guidance is:

> working towards a society in which there is a common vision and sense of belonging by all communities; a society in which the diversity of people's backgrounds and circumstances is appreciated and valued; a society in which similar life opportunities are available to all; and a society in which strong and positive relationships exist and continue to be developed in the workplace, in schools and in the wider community. (DCSF, 2007: 5)

There are four dimensions:

- the school community
- the community within which the school is located
- the UK community
- the global community.

Auditing for community cohesion

You should focus on:

- What does the school know about the community it serves?
- How has it used this to promote community cohesion and the needs of pupils?
- How does the school know it is successful?

In order to demonstrate how your schools measure up against the community cohesion expectations, use the following forms:

4.7, 4.8 & 4.9

- Online resource 4.7 'Community engagement, extended services audit'
- Online resource 4.8 'Teaching, learning and curriculum audit'
- Online resource 4.9 'Equity and excellence audit'.

The audit pages (4.7, 4.8 and 4.9) are designed to give school leaders and governors a brief overview of how different aspects of school life can contribute to the promotion of community cohesion.

The audits are designed to suit all phases of schools and should be adapted according to particular circumstances. A quick audit can be compiled by one member of staff in preparation for a briefing meeting or discussion amongst a group, some of whom have good knowledge of what is going on in the school. In some schools, a wider group will be brought together to conduct the audit.

Next to each descriptor there are two additional columns, a larger one to make an initial note and a smaller one to 'flag' or highlight the item for further investigation or discussion. This audit has been designed with less to fill in than is usually the case so that it is not burdensome and can be conducted fairly quickly. Spaces are left at the end of each section for additional comment.

For schools wanting to collect more information during the audit, extra columns can be added before use. These might include more details about location and timing, the number and ages of pupils involved, the person responsible, a grading indicating how well established the work is, the location of any evidence, the cost implications and whether the item is regular or a 'one-off' event.

Alternatively a wider range of people could be selected to respond to the questions. This will take more time but would raise the awareness of a wider group about the promotion of community cohesion.

When the findings of the audit are brought together for discussion, some of the following questions could be discussed:

1 What areas of strength have emerged?
2 What evidence do we have? Is more evidence of strengths needed (e.g. for Ofsted)?
3 Have any interesting items come up that were not on the original audit sheets?
4 Were any significant gaps discovered?
5 What further information would be helpful before deciding on priorities for action? Do we need a more detailed audit of certain areas? Who should be involved in this?
6 Who else should be informed about these findings and how should this communication be done?
7 What are our immediate action points?

For more information on community cohesion and inspection see Chapter 10.

Self-evaluation questions for the ESC

You might use the Figure 4.5 to check on your own level of development and support for community cohesion (available as online resource 4.10). These questions can act as pointers for further development of provision.

4.10

How do you check on the balance of activities the pupils are accessing? Are some groups insufficiently represented? How do you address this?	
How are you attempting to gather the views of and work with hard-to-reach parents? Do you consult with all groups of parents and take their views into account?	
Is there understanding within the school of the meaning of community and do you try to spread this understanding where possible?	
Do the range of activities on offer reflect the diversity of groups within the school?	
Is information for parents presented in a manner accessible to different groups?	
Are different groups consulted? Have their views been acted on?	
Does extended provision show a responsiveness to the needs of families locally?	
To what extent do extra-curricular activities encourage understanding of others' lives?	

Figure 4.5 Self-evaluation questions for the ESC

Online resource 4.11 provides information on completing the evaluation schedule.

Table 4.2 provides practical examples of some of the activities that schools have included in order to promote community cohesion, collated here from examples provided by DCSF, as detailed on the Teachernet Website. This small sample can be used to demonstrate a range of possibilities. 4.11

To find out further information regarding these case studies or to see them in full visit www.teachernet.gov.uk/wholeschool/Communitycohesion/Community_cohesion_case_studies/.

Table 4.2 Community cohesion case studies

Guidance to promote community cohesion	Teaching, learning and curriculum
Explore different cultures, ethnicity or religions – by school linking	Inclusive transitions and sharing identities – between countries
Engaging parents – by establishing a parents group	Children learning with and from each other – between different cultures
Building pupil and parent involvement – using parent programmes	Twinning project – using visits, sports, arts and celebrating religious festivals
Discover hidden aspects and connections – pairs of schools – working with university experts	Community cohesion – exploring the local community
Reducing violence and vandalism – working with different organizations and individuals to enhance the community environment	Subject-based or cross-curricular cohesion issues – using themed days (every 16th day)
Addressing barriers to learning – improving community relations by working with local and national schemes	Introduce different areas and cultures within Britain and beyond – using the Flying Carpet
Parent involvement – initiatives to encourage parents to support their children's early years development	Pupils leading social cohesion – pupil-lead research project into 'What differences do we celebrate, tolerate or find difficult' across the local authority
Teaching pupils to value diversity – within a multi-cultural area using adult and family learning activities	Teacher exchanges – using a Chinese teacher at the school annually, who teaches language, promotes cross-curricular links to art, music, geography and PSHE
Engaging with parents and the local community – through extended services	

Equity and excellence	Engagement and extended services
Students have a democratic voice, fostering cohesion from within – Pupils Equal Opportunity Policy	Looking at historical and geographical connections – school linking
Raising self-esteem of Roma pupils – and the profile of the pupils within the school and wider community	Break down stereotypes and promote dialogue – using inter-generational activities
Capturing imagination and raising attainment of Gypsy, Roma and Traveller children	Remove barriers to access and participation – parental support and personalized learning
Creating a sense of family identity – shift in school culture to embrace different communities	Celebrates differences and similarities within school local community – intergenerational project
Ethnic minority achievement particularly of black and mixed heritage boys – using senior staff role models	Promote and celebrate diversity within the school – use family history and movement
Raising achievement through emotional intelligence – use different initiatives and build on that learning by improving transition between school phases	Build resilience, counter terrorism and prevent young people joining gangs and being involved in gun crime – evening mentoring project
Whole-school learning – taking a whole-school approach to teaching pupils with English as an additional language and engaging with the community	Promoting good relations – using theatre, arts and story telling
	Developing social skills – community-based initiatives for pupils and their parents
	Raising ethnic minority achievement – through a matrix of outreach and support services

5 Finding out what's available

Chapter aims

- To help you identify the groups and organizations that may be useful
- To identify complementary initiatives
- To locate useful sources of information
- To help you develop your directory in conjunction with your schools

Topics

- Groups and organizations that can help
- Complementary initiatives
- Sources of information
- School use

Figure

- 5.1 Services audit

Tables

- 5.1 Finding out about local groups
- 5.2 Other services
- 5.3 Core offer initiatives
- 5.4 Website information

- 5.5 Electronic newsletters
- 5.6 Magazines

Online resources

- 5.1 Services audit

You are not on your own. In fact it is more likely that you will be astounded by the vast number of organizations, programmes, projects and groups that exist in order to support, educate, manage and innovate. Public, private and voluntary sector – the difficulty can be familiarizing yourself with what's available. However, this must be a major part of your role.

Groups and organizations that can help

Where there is a need, help and support groups are not usually far behind. British society has a tendency to want to form groups with common aims and shared experiences. These can often be a very useful source of advice and information, particularly when you come across a new illness, addiction or family circumstance that you've not met before. Many of these organizations will have charity status and are voluntary organizations. You will have to familiarize yourself with the local 'directory'. Table 5.1 identifies some places you might go to find out about local groups and services.

Table 5.1 Finding out about local groups

Source	Information
Community forums or locality meetings	Hosted by the local authority and police and held in community venues. They may well be aware of different community groups
Community and voluntary service	Details about community groups, i.e. Caribbean Resident's Association, Polish Community Groups
Residents associations	Visit groups to discover information about local community groups
Local libraries	Libraries will often be used by the emerging groups or details might be advertised there
Local community centre	Visit community centres as these are used by community groups

There are numerous organizations that you can team up with for support. These include statutory organizations, community and voluntary organizations, local clubs and private companies. Table 5.2 is a list of the main areas where support can be gained and examples of how these services could be used have been included. However, all these services could be engaged in joint projects, if they have the capacity.

Table 5.2 Other services

Statutory agencies	
Primary care trust	Working on joint projects, i.e. MEND or Smoking Cessation
Local authority transport dept	Assistance for rural projects over holidays
Family support workers	Signposting towards services or assistance with consultation
School nurses	Could run awareness or drop-in sessions for pupils or parents
Children's centres	Working on joint projects, signposting, hiring rooms for community venue
Police community support officers	Working on joint projects, signposting to services
Anti-bullying coordinator	Assistance around anti-bullying weeks and to signpost to services
Sexual health services	Attendance at events for parents or signposting to services
Job centre	Attendance at events, signposting to services
Youth and community services	Joint projects, i.e. summer activities or signposting towards their services
Heritage education (inc. libraries)	Often run activities for pupils and parents in holidays
Speech and language therapy	Signposting to their services
Youth offending team.	Run parenting programmes to signpost towards

Table 5.2 Other services *continued*

Community and voluntary organizations	
St John's Ambulance	Running first aid courses or signposting towards their badgers and cadets
Residents associations	Work with during consultation and community events. Some have newsletters
Boys clubs	Running joint projects, hiring their venue or signposting to their activities
Community youth clubs	Running joint projects or signposting to their services
Housing associations	Signposting to services
Bereavement support	Signposting to services
Scouts and girl guides	Often run sessions in the community – signpost or set up new groups
Counselling services	Signpost to services or work together on joint projects
Separation and loss services	Signposting to services
Credit unions	Often run collection points in schools
Citizens Advice Bureau	Signposting to services or working on joint projects (i.e. financial capability)
Community cafes	Hold community information and adult learning sessions
Museums	Often run activities for community – signpost towards
Private organizations	
FE colleges	Delivering adult learning or signposting to provision
Leisure trusts	Working on joint projects or signposting to their leisure activities
Private training providers	Delivering adult learning or signposting to provision
Local radio	Useful to promote events or have to come along to fun days etc.

Complementary initiatives

There is no shortage of programmes, initiatives or projects available to schools. They should be complementary to the work that you do. Table 5.3 provides some of the main ones you might encounter.

Table 5.3 Core offer initiatives

Core offer	Examples of other initiatives
Childcare	Children's centres* Sure Start* Family support workers Tax credits*
Varied menu of activities	School Sports Partnership* Sports club links* Healthy schools* Eco-Schools* Learning outside the classroom manifesto and quality badge Positive Activities for Young People* Youth and community service School Food Trust Artsmark*
Parenting support	Parent support advisors* Transition information sessions* Youth offending teams Safer Schools Partnerships*
Adult learning	Skills for Life* Family learning Lifelong learning Financial literacy

Table 5.3 Core offer initiatives *continued*

Core offer	Examples of other initiatives
Swift and easy access	Learning mentors School nurse Education social workers Teenage pregnancy and sexual health Obesity programmes (PCT) Child and adolescent mental health services Speech and language therapy
Community access	Job Centre Plus Citizens Advice Bureau New Deal* Building Schools for the Future* Specialist status*

*More information about these programmes is included below.

Sure Start Children's Centres

Sure Start is the government's programme to bring together early education, childcare, health and family support. Sure Start Children's Centres build on existing initiatives such as Sure Start Local Programmes, Neighbourhood Nurseries and Early Excellence Centres to integrate early years services in communities.

The centres cater for children under five years old and their families. Although they vary according to centre, they might include:

- integrated early education and childcare;
- support for parents – including advice on parenting, local childcare options and access to specialist services;
- child and family health services;
- helping parents into work.

Tax credits

Tax credits are available for those paying tax who also have children and for those earning low wages. The amount of tax credits depends on:

- how many children you have living with you;
- how many hours you work;
- the cost of childcare;
- if you or any child living with you has a disability;
- if you're aged fifty-plus and are coming off benefits.

The lower your income the more tax credits you will receive. More information is available at www.direct.gov.uk.

School Sport Partnerships (SSPs)

SSPs are groups of schools working together to develop PE and sport opportunities for young people. A partnership might consist of:

- a partnership development manager (PDM);
- up to eight school sport coordinators (SSCos);
- forty-five primary and special school link teachers (PLTs).

The PDM is a full-time role usually based within a sports college. They manage the partnership. An SSCo is based in a secondary school and concentrates on improving school sport opportunities across a family of schools. PLTs are based in primary and special schools and aim to improve the quantity and quality of PE and sport in their own schools.

School sport club links

A school–club link is an agreement between a school or school sport partnership and a community-based sports club to work together. This includes multi-skills clubs and dance links. The aim is for young people to participate in club activities for at least one to three hours per week.

Healthy schools

The National Healthy Schools Programme aims are to:

- support children and young people in developing healthy behaviours;
- help raise the achievement of children and young people;
- help reduce health inequalities;
- help promote social inclusion.

The government set a target for all schools to be participating in the programme by 2009 and 75 per cent to have achieved National Healthy School Status.

There are ten elements to the whole-school approach:

- Leadership, management and managing change
- Policy development
- Curriculum planning and work with outside agencies
- Teaching and learning
- School culture and environment
- Giving children and young people a voice
- Provision of pupil support services
- Staff professional development needs, health and welfare
- Partnerships with parents/carers and local communities
- Assessing recording and reporting children and young peoples' achievement.

It has four themes:

- Personal, Social and Health Education including Sex and Relationship Education (SRE) and Drug Education (including alcohol, tobacco and volatile substance abuse)
- Healthy eating
- Physical activity
- Emotional health and well-being, including bullying.

All schools achieving National Healthy School Status must have met national criteria using a whole-school approach across the four core themes. Schools identify needs and necessary actions through an audit. Schools then self-validate when they are sure the criteria are met and minimum evidence is in place with outcomes recorded.

Eco-Schools

The government wants all schools to be sustainable schools by 2020. Eco-Schools is an international award programme run by the Foundation for Environmental Education (FEE). Schools register to join and then follow a seven-step process which helps them to address a variety of environmental themes from litter and waste to healthy living and biodiversity.

Children lead an eco-committee and help carry out an audit to assess the environmental performance of their school. The pupils decide which environmental themes they want to address. Schools work towards one of three awards – Bronze, Silver and the Green Flag award.

Positive Activities for Young People

This programme is aimed at 8–19 year olds who are at risk of social exclusion and community crime. It includes diversionary and developmental activities during school holidays.

Artsmark

Artsmark is a national award scheme managed by the Arts Council. It recognizes schools with a high level of provision in the arts including art, dance, drama and music. The application form acts as an auditing tool and is also designed to raise awareness for the school of the quality and quantity of provision available.

Schools can achieve the Artsmark, Artsmark Silver and Artsmark Gold. The award is valid for three years.

The parent support advisor project

A two-year pilot programme involving twenty local authorities developed the parent support advisor (PSA) role. Subsequently there is further commitment towards expanding the PSA role in schools with the DCSF pledging further funding for training and to help local authorities with its implementation.

The aims of the PSA is to work with parents in the school context with a focus on improving behaviour and attendance and overcoming barriers to learning. It is intended that the PSA will help to increase the number of parents involved in their child's education.

Transition information sessions (TIS)

These sessions are for parents during transition between schools. They are part of the core parenting support element of the extended services offer. They include giving parents information about the range of services available to support them. All schools are expected to offer transition information sessions to parents by 2010.

Safer Schools Partnership

This programme aims to provide a joined-up approach to crime prevention by placing police in schools. Safer School Partnerships (SSPs) have been established in some schools in areas with high levels of street crime. There are currently around 400 SSPs running and it is the government's intention to extend the scheme. The Youth Crime Action Plan 2008 recommends the spread of SSPs and promotes the entitlement of parents to request that one is established in their child's school.

SSPs aim to improve relationships between young people and the police, promoting school safety and reducing risk of crime and antisocial behaviour. As part of this drive to improve the links between schools and the police the Youth Crime Action Plan states that every school will have a named police contact.

Skills for Life

Skills for Life qualifications are designed to help adults develop the skills that are necessary in everyday life such as reading, writing and maths. They are aimed at adults over 16 years of age who have left compulsory full-time education and do not have a basic English or maths qualification. Skills for Life certificates are available in adult literacy, numeracy and ICT.

New Deal

This programme is aimed at those on jobseeker's allowance in order for them to continue to receive benefits. It aims to improve skills in order to help them find and keep a job or start work for themselves.

Building Schools for the Future

Through this programme it is intended to rebuild or renew every secondary school in England. It is expected that these new schools will provide twenty-first-century teaching and learning facilities for all secondary pupils and staff. There is a revised national programme available at www.teachernet.gov.uk.

Specialist status

Specialist status is intended to raise standards in secondary education. Around 90 per cent of maintained secondary schools are now specialist. The specialist school programme is designed to help schools in partnership with private sector sponsors and supported by additional government funding to establish chosen specialisms. These include arts, business and enterprise, engineering, humanities, languages, mathematics and computing, music, science, sports and technology.

Schools can also combine any two specialisms. Special schools can apply for an SEN specialism in one of the four areas of the SEN code of practice.

Sources of information

Numerous places can be used to find information about what is available. Tables 5.4, 5.5 and 5.6 identify possible sources of information from websites, newsletters and magazines.

Table 5.4 Website information

Website	Details	URL
ContinYou	A charity that aims to open up opportunities for learning	www.continyou.org.uk
TDA	A public body that aims to raise standards in schools through training and development	www.tda.gov.uk
Teachernet	A government website for teachers and school-related professions	www.teachernet.gov.uk
Direct Gov	A government website with information on childcare, education, etc.	www.direct.gov.uk
Teachers TV	A website with videos which can be used as resources	www.teachers.tv
Every Child Matters	Government website with information regarding the framework	www.everychildmatters.gov.uk
4 Children	A national children's charity	www.4children.org.uk
DCSF	Department for Children, Schools and Families	www.dcsf.gov.uk
NIACE	National Institute of Adult Continuing Education	www.niace.org.uk
Infed	Resource for those interested in informal education, youth work, community development and lifelong learning	www.infed.org
NC	National College for Leadership of Schools and Children's Serices	www.nationalcollege.org.uk
NCVYS	National Council for Voluntary Youth Service	www.ncvys.org.uk
Ofsted	Inspectors – website contains inspection reports	www.ofsted.gov.uk

Table 5.5 Electronic newsletters

Electronic newsletter	Details	URL
DCSF Latest News and Publications	All the latest news and access to recent publications	www.dcsf.gov.uk
Teachers TV Newsletter	Weekly newsletter, highlighting the topics in focus	www.teachers.tv
ContinYou Breakfast Bulletin Newsletter	A monthly newsletter with news, funding, menus, activities and campaigns	www.continyou.org
BBC Campaigns (Blast, RAW)	Various educational related campaigns from the BBC	www.bbc.co.uk
Community and Voluntary Action (CVS)	Weekly updates from this local service. Find your local branch from the national website	www.navca.org.uk
TDA Deliver	A bulletin containing news, resources and events	www.tda.gov.uk
Children and Young People Now, Daily Bulletin	Highlighting the top stories affecting the sector, in the daily breaking news bulletin	www.cypnow.co.uk
Children and Young People Now 'In Practice'	Aimed at people involved with children's centres or extended services. It is produced in conjunction with 4children and ContinYou and sent weekly	www.cypnow.co.uk

Table 5.6 Magazines

Magazines	Details
Schools Etc	Continyou
Children and Young People Daily	Haymarket Business Subscriptions
Local Authority Magazines	Contact your local authority
Touchbase	Department for Work and Pensions

School use

You should by now be building your own directory of available support networks and groups. The next stage is to check the extent to which your schools are using them or are even aware of their existence. You could use Figure 5.1 to enter into discussions with your schools about what they currently access, signpost or host (also available as online resource 5.1).

5.1

Statutory services	School is aware of this service	School signposts to this service	Service has a presence in school	School would like more information about this service	School would like involvement with the service
Speech and Language Services					
Educational Psychologist					
Behavioural Support Team					
Primary Mental Health Team					
Child and Family Therapy					
Educational Social Workers					
Children's Centres					
Occupational Therapy					
Family Support Workers					
Behavioural Support Services					
Social Services					
Police Community Support Officers					
Integrated Disability Support					
Child and Adolescent Mental Health Services (CAMHS)					
Positive about Young People					
Youth and Community Service					
Job Centre					
Anti-Bullying					
Sexual Health Services					

This audit will help to understand the services that are currently used by the local schools and determine any areas where further services are required.

Community and voluntary services	School is aware of this service	School signposts to this service	Service has a presence in school	School would like more information about service	School would like more involvement with the service
Relate					
Counselling Services					
Drug and Alcohol Services					
Housing Association					
Sexual Health Services					
Youth Organizations					
Domestic Violence Services					
Peer Mentoring Services					
Smoking Cessation					
Bereavement Support					
Separation and Loss Services					
Carer Support Groups					
Healthy Living Network					
Credit Union					

Figure 5.1 Services audit

6 Signposting and publicity

Chapter aims

- To consider what is meant by 'signposting'
- To identify different ways of publicizing your provision
- To consider the benefits and disadvantages of different methods of communicating

Topics

- Signposting
- Creating an extended services signposting folder
- Signposting pamphlets and leaflets
- Newsletters
- Notice and presentation boards
- Email and websites
- Using the media
- Using yourself
- Pros and cons

Figure

- 6.1 Notifying the press

Tables

Online resources

Developing extended services provision does not mean every school providing the whole of the core offer. This would not be possible or beneficial. However, within a local community every service should be available and accessible to those people who need them. The extended services coordinator has a crucial role in trying to ensure that each school in the cluster either provides the service or can 'signpost' parents to where they can access it. Making sure that people know what is available, where and when is crucial to developing the range of services between schools.

Signposting

Your research into the available activities and services will have lead you to many meetings with partners and visits to community venues to obtain information and form relationships. This research is essential to ensure that the activities and services you create are not duplicated, but essentially will have assisted you in creating an accurate picture of what is available locally.

This knowledge will prove beneficial as you might be asked for a particular service by a headteacher, staff member or parent and the signposting towards existing provision is appropriate. It is often the case that there are a plethora of activities and services taking place in the community, but that schools and parents are unaware of their existence.

When creating signposting materials for schools, including leaflets and even newsletters for parents, you might want to photocopy the first one that you create for the schools, but then email the original for them to copy. How the item is used is at the discretion of each school and will often differ depending on the value that schools feel the material will have for their parents. Some schools will photocopy leaflets automatically; others might put it on their noticeboard or website. Many schools include it within their own school newsletter or put a note telling parents they can collect a copy from their school. Your job is to create the signposting material to ensure that the children, young people and families have the best opportunity of accessing the information through different formats. It is each school's individual decision as to how these are used.

You are the holder of a vast quantity of information. But how do you transfer that knowledge to the people who need it most? You will need to identify the most effective ways of reaching and communicating with your different groups. Table 6.1 provides some suggestions.

Table 6.1 Types of publicity – who and how

Audience	**Means of reaching**
Parents coming on to school premises on a daily basis	• Extended services signposting folder • Reception area displays and areas for leaflets • TV or touch-screen to advertise the services on offer • Parents' room directories and posters • Coffee mornings • Out on the playground • Community information file • Noticeboard
Parents attending selected school events	• Signposting pamphlets • Temporary stall or presentation board • One-to-one approach • Noticeboard
Parents who rarely visit the school	• Website • Leaflets in public places and at other venues • Letters taken home by pupils
Other members of the community	• Website • Leaflets in public places and at other venues • Community information file
School pupils	• Assemblies • School council • Holiday activity leaflets • Activity newsletters

6.9 More information is provided in online resource 6.9 'Publicizing what you do'.

Creating an extended services signposting folder

Much of your publicity will come in the form of bulletins, newsletters and flyers. However, with more than one school, you will not be able to provide signposting information in all your schools at the point when it is needed. This is why you might want to consider developing an extended services folder which can allow members of school staff to find the right organization or group for parents requesting information at the time.

A lose-leaf ring binder is probably most appropriate as the information in the folder will need amending at intervals. You might request that the folder is kept in reception – a good place for parents to browse whilst they are waiting for members of staff or children.

You might wish to include some inserts of your own with particular references to services or just include selections of leaflets and flyers produced by the organizations themselves. Either way it should be made clear that leaflets should not be removed and that you cannot guarantee the quality of all the services on offer.

The maintenance of the folder can be difficult. Ideally, you will want to update the folders every term. This will probably involve you collecting them and making any alterations. If you are lucky you might have a contact within the school office who is prepared to do this for you.

Some schools may already have a signposting folder, but not necessarily kept for parents to access. These schools may ask for the information to be sent to them, for adding to their folder, such as childcare information, parenting courses, etc.

Signposting pamphlets and leaflets

Creating your own leaflets and pamphlets can be a very flexible way of advertising particular aspects of your provision (online resource 6.10). You can hand these out at parents' evenings, during community events and when visiting community 6.10

groups. You might ask schools for permission to distribute leaflets to parents at the school gate. Many schools may have a section in their reception area which has pockets for leaflets, flyers and pamphlets. Information could be sent to these schools for display.

Alternatively you could collect a selection of leaflets from your community travels and group them together under the following headings: varied menu (online resource 6.3 'Varied menu'), swift and easy access and adult learning. These can be handy to produce at parents' evenings, depending on the evening's focus (online resource 6.4 'Parent evening themes').

6.3 & 6.4

You might want to be a little more ambitious and bring information together in a pamphlet which signposts the core offer and includes local activities and services that are taking place. The scope of such a publication could only extend to basic information such as organization names and telephone numbers. You could aim to cover the whole of the core offer, or put them into themes such as learning and advice services (see online resource 6.5 'Local community advice').

You might have leaflets to promote the activities and services available at a particular school. For example, online resource 6.7 'Core offer school'.

6.5 & 6.7

Newsletters

Having a regular input into a newsletter or creating your own can be a very useful way of keeping your community informed. Most schools have their own newsletter and it is beneficial for you to know when these go out. You will need to be clear:

- what the deadline for any contributions is;
- how much space you can have;
- to whom and in what form your contribution should be handed in to.

You might also be able to contribute to community newsletters. For example, local residents' associations, community centres and religious groups might have newsletters of their own that you could submit to. Be careful not to commit yourself to too many regular bulletins that you are going to find difficult to honour.

Alternatively you could create your own. The benefit of this is that you can tailor it to your own requirements. However, you must be cautious about taking on too much. Consider carefully the frequency of your newsletter. More than once a month is probably not feasible. However, creating one to email to all your schools and organizations can be considerably easier that contributing to theirs. Once you have established a pro forma it can be quite easy to amend monthly. See the example parent newsletter in online resource 6.8. 6.8

It is also likely that where there are particular projects that schools and groups are running, they will promote them themselves in their own newsletters.

Holiday activity leaflets

There might be times when you particularly want to highlight some new provision or a range of activities during holiday times.

During these times parents will want to know what is the menu of possible activities. It can be difficult to signpost to everything individually and the range of activities available might best be covered in one leaflet or publication.

You will need to send a holiday activity leaflet in advance to schools giving as much notice as possible but not so early that there is time to lose or forget about it. Ideally, you might also be able to publicize the leaflet itself during an assembly or summer term parents' evening (see online resource 6.2 'Easter 6.2
activities leaflet').

If you are able to engage with partners and sponsors you might be able to go slightly grander and produce an A5-size holiday activity booklet (online resource 6.1
6.1 'Holiday booklet'). The schools might need to contribute some start-up costs or you might need to apply for funding. However, selling advertising space may well cover the costs.

Notice and presentation boards

Noticeboards provide a static opportunity to display a flyer or poster for a period of time. Most schools and community groups will use some form of board to post bulletins to their community. Any poster you submit needs to be eye-catching and contain the basic information needed to advertise your activity with a contact number or details to enable interested parties to find out more. Don't overload posters with too much information. Readers will either not bother to read it all or will forget it anyway. You might want to consider having the contact details on a tear away strip that people can rip off and take with them rather than needing to write down the details. Depending on space, some schools might be prepared to give you a permanent notice board of your own. Where this happens, it is an additional task that you must build into your week.

Schools are an obvious venue, but you should also look further afield into the community to distribute your posters. Children's centres, libraries, one-stop shops, community cafes and local leisure centres might all welcome your publications. You might also ask local shops and supermarkets to display your posters.

An alternative is to put together your own portable noticeboard that you can take with you for display at busy times in different venues. Beg, borrow or buy a presentation board and decorate this with laminated signposting information. Take this to parents' evenings to highlight the partners providing services and activities taking place in the school. It will draw attention to you and your role and hopefully make people inquisitive enough to want to find out more. Depending on your budget you might hire a market stall or stand in a shopping centre for a day, taking your posters and leaflets.

Email and websites

For those who have it, the internet provides an immediate and easy to use tool and is one that can be of great benefit to you. Through using email you can quickly attach and send your newsletters and posters to all your saved contacts. These should include schools, faith groups, family information services, community centres, colleges, housing associations and voluntary organizations. Provided they have an efficient method of dealing with mail, this is as good a method as any of sending out your literature. Your school might enable you to email parents or use group texting to send messages about events and courses.

Schools and groups vary as to the extent they have developed a website. In some cases there is an advanced website with constantly updated pages; in others, nothing at all. At the least, where schools do have websites, you will want to ensure that they include reference to you, your role and how you might be contacted. At the most you might be allowed to prepare some of your own web pages for the school site. You could use these to signpost to services within the school or the community.

Other websites could also be accessible to you. Your local authority might host website events or there might be opportunity for you to use the council's website. Local groups sometimes have their own websites and www.netmums.com can be useful wherever you are.

Alternatively, depending on your resources, level of expertise and support available, you might want to create a specific extended services website for the cluster or the geographical area. You might need to obtain funding for this – see Chapter 8. Sample website pages can be found in the online resources 6.11 'Homepage' and 6.12 'Core offer'. 6.11 & 6.12

Keep the structure and format of your website/page simple with limited use of graphics. You should try to maintain a consistency of presentation throughout avoiding frames that will not fit an A4 page when it is printed. Be aware of copyright laws when importing images and photographs and be careful about using images of children. Children's names and pictures can be published, but not together.

Websites can only be useful where they are regularly updated. Once you have a web page, you have committed yourself to its maintenance.

Using the media

Local radio stations and newspapers rely upon local services and facilities to keep them in touch with what's happening. Any good publicity you can attract for your schools will be appreciated. In many cases a member of the school staff will already have the responsibility of alerting the press to news opportunities. If this is the case, all you need to do is let the member of staff (usually in the office) know what is happening and when. It is beneficial to write down for them a summary of the activity you wish to draw attention to. Figure 6.1 provides an example.

Date and time of event:	Purpose of event:
Who it is aimed at:	Any unusual/ news worthy features:
Contact details:	Opportunities for a photograph:

Figure 6.1 Notifying the press

From this it might be that a photographer will attend the event, take pictures and that you will be contacted by telephone to provide some of the details. You will need to make sure that any children included in a photograph have parental permission for this. The school will usually have a list of any children who should not be included in photographs and you must liaise with them.

Your local authority press office can be a mine of useful information and a great support if problems emerge. They can help you spread the word and introduce you to the council's own publications. They might have guidance on writing a press release or might even work with you on writing one. You should contact them to find out what support they offer.

Local radio can also be very interested in local stories. Similar to the newspapers, have the essential information written down before hand and make sure you give them plenty of notice. Much can depend on what else is happening that week.

Using yourself

You are your own best advocate. Meeting with you is the most direct method likely to enthuse members of your community. Your enthusiasm and commitment can be infectious and make all the difference to the extent to which schools and other organizations will 'buy in' to the extended services concept.

Therefore, although using paper and the internet can be very good ways of letting people know what's going on, your own personal touch is precious. You should aim to be recognizable within your community. Although time-consuming, it is beneficial to be able to introduce yourself in as many places as possible. Of course, this does have its disadvantages. The parent who stops you on the street when you are in the middle of doing your shopping or the individual who quizzes you at length about the assessment practices at such and such school. These interruptions are part and parcel of the role you hold and must be treated as such.

The personal contacts that you make will give you highly beneficial insight into your community. It can be very difficult to acquire this in any other way than getting out and about to meet the very people who you are developing services for.

Out on the playground

Try to spend time in playgrounds. Before school and at the end of the school day are ripe times for meeting parents of primary school pupils. You will also get a feel at these times for the ethos of the school. Seeing pupils in the playground and hearing their parents chat can provide real insight into school issues and areas for development.

You might just informally walk round clusters of parents introducing yourself or you could set up a little stall during the summer months. Depending on facilities and time, you could even provide some refreshments in an adjacent classroom and invite parents in to meet with you and share their suggestions for additional facilities and services they might appreciate.

At break time, spending time in the playground is a useful way of chatting to pupils to find out what they would like to have on offer and how they feel about the existing activities provided. Check with school staff before doing this.

Assemblies

Having a five minute slot in assembly can be beneficial for reaching the maximum number of staff and children at the same time. Even better if it is an assembly that parents are invited to. You should aim to attend assemblies as often as you can and suggest that course and activities providers do the same. Some people can find it intimidating. However, school staff will usually welcome a 'visitors' assembly and will be supportive of anyone wishing to have a go.

If you have chance, check before hand with a member of school staff what you are planning to do. It is always beneficial to include something visual if you can and children love it if you involve them in some way on stage. So, for example, if you are advertising a family cookery course at primary school you might bring one of them on the stage to dress in a chef's hat and apron (a poster for a cookery course is provided in online resource 6.6).

6.6

Schools council

Each of your schools will have a method of listening to the pupil voice. Usually this is in the form of a school's council. If you are finding it difficult to make assembly time, you might spread your message and advertise your activities through this group. Take leaflets along (check how many representatives are likely to be attending) and ask council members to take them back to their class and display. It is ideal if you can present a new activity in an assembly and then follow it up by addressing the school council.

Outside the school

Much of what you do will be located within your schools. However, it is clear that your role is about extending into and working with the community. This can only happen if you are also prepared to venture outside the school gates and introduce yourself in other local venues.

This could include visiting social and religious groups and residents' associations. However, if you also want to meet those who perhaps do not belong to any particular group, hiring a market stall or stand in a shopping centre for the day can be beneficial. Take a selection of leaflets, posters and freebies, if you can, to open up discussions with people without having the influence of anyone's agenda.

Holding events

You might want to run an open day or taster session to attract audiences. This would give you the chance to advertise everything at the same time and hopefully demonstrate that there is something for everyone available. With the opportunity to talk to your community, you can both sell and consult.

You will need to find a method of attracting people to attend in the first place, so carefully consider your site and time. Perhaps use a theme such as 'pampering' to attract audiences and the media. You can invite partner services to the event to set up their own stall and showcase the services they provide. Refreshments and a bouncy castle can help attract both parents and children. A school's autumn or summer fayre provide an excellent opportunity for you to piggy back an event. See if you can have your own 'corner' or room in which to advertise the extended services provision locally. Liaising with the school's PTA or 'Friends of…' will help you to identify this kind of opportunity and it is likely that they will appreciate your involvement.

Pros and cons

Whichever form of publicity or signposting you choose, there will be accompanying benefits and disadvantages. For this reason, the best approach is to take a mixed one. Try not to rely too heavily on one outlet and be prepared to vary your approaches with your audience in mind. Be receptive to people's suggestions and don't be too downhearted if something you try is a flop. Just experimenting with different times, venues and presentation will mean sometimes you get it right and sometimes wrong. Word of mouth remains an extremely powerful form of communication. Just one member of your community who you have chance to speak to and 'convert' can make an impression on several more. Nurture each opportunity and you are doing as much as can be expected of you. Table 6.2 provides some pros and cons of different types of communication.

Table 6.2 Communication pros and cons

Type of communication	**Pros**	**Cons**
Newsletter	Easy to administer Will have a large audience	Not everyone reads them Need a regular commitment
Poster	Easy to administer Eye-catching in the right place	Need constant replacement – they soon become wallpaper
Email website	Easy and quick to administer – you can have a very wide circulation at the click of a button	Not everyone regularly opens their email or has the facility to view a website – can have the effect of limiting your users
Face-to-face	A wonderful opportunity to really get to know what's going on and explain in detail what you are doing You are much more likely to get people involved	Very time-consuming Can be difficult to get to the people you really want to
Pamphlets and booklets	Excellent way of ensuring you have all the information in one place Can be used as a reference by other school staff when you're not there	Time-consuming to produced Need frequent updating
Newspapers	Reach a large audience and give your schools a welcome profile in the community	Need to think well-ahead to organize Need to check on permission for photographs etc.

7 Practicalities

Chapter aims

- To identify how an extended services coordinator might be involved in safeguarding procedures
- To explain what a Common Assessment Framework is and how it works
- To help clarify what you should do in case of disclosure
- To outline some implications for recruitment of staff and volunteers
- To help you recognize health and safety issues
- To help you ensure that you meet equal opportunities requirements

Topics

- Safeguarding
- Health and safety
- Equality and diversity

Figure

Tables

Online resources

- 7.1 Record of concerns
- 7.2 Signs of abuse
- 7.3 Health and safety – further information
- 7.4 Sample lettings policy
- 7.5 Example risk assessment
- 7.6 Checklist for clubs

You will have lots of ambitions and high expectations for what you would like to achieve as extended services coordinator. Some of your projects will be particularly exciting and you will be keen to get them underway. However, you will also come across numerous hurdles. Some of these will be linked to staffing issues, others to health and safety. This chapter looks at the practicalities of the job and aims to help you ensure that you can follow the correct policies and procedures without letting them grind you down.

Safeguarding

Child protection is part of safeguarding and promoting the welfare of children. The definition given by the DCSF is:

- promoting children from maltreatment
- preventing impairment of children's health or development
- ensuring that children are growing up in circumstances consistent with the provision of safe and effective care
- and undertaking that role so as to enable those children to have optimum life chances and to enter adulthood successfully. (2006: 34–5)

The extended services coordinator has a key role in this process. Effective safeguarding is very much dependent upon agencies working together and sharing information. ESCs can form the link between services and provide the access that parents and professionals need to protect the well-being of the child.

In the document 'Every Child Matters: Change for Children', the outcome 'Stay Safe' is described as meaning:

- Safe from maltreatment, neglect, violence and sexual exploitation
- Safe from accidental injury and death
- Safe from bullying and discrimination
- Safe from crime and anti-social behaviour in and out of school
- Have security, stability and are cared for
- Parents, carers and families provide safe home and stability. (DfES, 2004: 9)

This does not mean that the other outcomes aren't also part of safeguarding. If pupils aren't supported in being healthy or if they aren't provided with opportunities for the future and their economic well-being, then we are not safeguarding them. 'Looking out for' our young people is an essential part of all children's services, amongst which the ESC has a central role.

All individuals working with children should be alert for signs of abuse and should be clear to whom they need to report any concerns. You will need to keep a note of the designated person responsible for child protection in each of your schools. In most cases this will be the headteacher. You should also create a method for recording any concerns you might have about an individual or one that has been reported to you. This record should show clearly what you do with the information you receive. It is better to speak to the designated person about an issue, however small it might seem, than to leave it unchecked only to find it is the tip of the iceberg. Table 7.1 identifies some of the headings you might want to use. A form template is provided as online resource 7.1. 7.1

Table 7.1 Record of concerns

Name of child	Date	Area of concern	Information shared with	Actions noted
Samantha Brown	22.05.2009	Since mum's new boyfriend has moved into the house Samantha has been reluctant to go home at the end of the day	Headteacher	Headteacher to contact mum and discuss concerns. Will monitor the situation.
	29.05.2009	Samantha seems to be more relaxed.		Meeting took place – headteacher reports mum agreed to spend more time with Samantha and be available when she comes home from school

Although Table 7.1 includes 'Actions noted' this does not mean that you necessarily need to action yourself. In most cases, once you have shared the information, the school's own child protection policy should take effect. However, an important element in safeguarding is that it is a community responsibility. Problems occasionally arise because individuals simply want to pass on information rather than also taking some responsibility for seeing it followed through. It is quite reasonable to ask what is being done following a referral to the designated person. If you are not happy with the response, you can contact Children's Social Care direct.

The Common Assessment Framework

It is unlikely that an ESC will need to participate in social care meetings linked to a particular family. However, they might be asked to contribute towards a Common Assessment Framework (CAF).

The CAF is a central part of the ECM agenda. It is designed to enable the early identification of needs in order to mobilize services and ensure their needs are met. The CAF form of assessment is a holistic approach that requires multi-agency work. The relevant services include health, schools (including independent schools), further education colleges, youth support services/Connexions, childcare, early years, social care, police and youth justice.

Three steps to producing a CAF are outlined below. You will not need to implement these yourself.

- *Step 1: Preparation.* This involves recognizing potential needs and then discussing the situation with the child, involving parents or carers unless this is not appropriate. It is important to find out whether a common assessment already exists. After reviewing the existing information a practitioner decides whether to undertake a common assessment with the agreement of the child or family, as appropriate.
- *Step 2: Discussion.* This involves completing the assessment with the child and family, making use of information already gathered from the child, family or other practitioners, and completing a consent statement. At the end of the discussion, the practitioner should better understand the child's needs and what can be done to help.
- *Step 3: Delivery.* This involves agreeing actions that the practitioner's service or the family can deliver, and considering what may be needed from other services. Note: the CAF does not give a practitioner the ability to guarantee a service from another organization without consulting that organization. It is important that practitioners have a good knowledge of local services and how they operate.

The ESC might be involved in working with social services and the school to identify agencies which will be able to support and work with a family on the needs identified during a CAF. It could be beneficial for the ESC to attend CAF training to familiarize themselves with the system and paperwork. The ESC could also attend 'area partnership' meetings to work closer with the local authority CAF personnel.

Categories of abuse

All school personnel must be vigilant for signs of abuse. The following is guidance as to the types of abuse that might be encountered (also see online resource 7.2 'Signs of abuse'). 7.2

Abuse might include:

- *Physical*. This can involve hitting and shaking, throwing, poisoning, burning or scalding or otherwise causing physical harm to a child. Physical harm can also be caused when a parent or carer fabricates the symptoms of, or deliberately induces, illness in a child.

- *Emotional*. This is the persistent emotional maltreatment of a child to the extent that there are severe and persistent adverse effects on the child's emotional development. This might include repeatedly telling a child they are worthless, having inappropriate expectations of them, letting them see or hear the maltreatment of another, serious bullying, the exploitation or corruption of children.

- *Sexual*. This involves forcing or enticing a child to take part in sexual activities. It might include prostitution, physical contact – both penetrative or non-penetrative – children looking at pornographic materials or watching sexual activities, encouraging children to behave in sexually inappropriate ways.

- *Neglect*. This is the most frequently used category of abuse and includes failure to provide sufficient food, clothing or shelter, failure to protect a child from physical and emotional harm or danger, failure to ensure adequate supervision or access to appropriate medical care.

Prolonged and/or regular exposure to domestic violence can also have serious impact on a child's development and emotional well-being.

Dealing with disclosure

It is vital that children are listened to and that what they have to say is taken seriously. During your time spent in environments with children and young people if a child does start to make a disclosure, they should not be questioned too closely but should be allowed the opportunity to talk. As soon as is possible, a referral should be made to the designated person with any details of the disclosure dated and signed. You should remember:

- never to promise to keep what is said a secret;

- that concerns should be immediately reported to the designated person;

- that a written record should be kept which includes a record of the time, date, place and the names of anyone else present;

- it is not your role to investigate but accept what the child says without challenge;

- to reassure the child that they are doing the right thing and that you recognize how hard it is for them;

- not to lay blame or criticize either the child or the perpetrator;
- if the designated person is not available, do not hesitate to make a referral yourself.

Listening to a disclosure can in itself be quite traumatic. You may also need to seek support from the appropriate school staff.

Checks on staff

The recruitment and monitoring practices of people working or volunteering with children comes under the Vetting and Barring Scheme. This involves the Independent Safeguarding Authority (ISA) who decide who is unsuitable to work or volunteer with vulnerable groups. It is illegal to hire someone who is not registered by the ISA.

It is important that recruiting employers take up references and scrutinize employment history. Volunteers as well as those employed must be ISA registered. The schools you work with will ultimately be responsible for managing this process. However, you will need to bear these requirements in mind when liaising with external providers, clubs and societies. Prospective volunteers and providers must be checked before they can start volunteering or engage in a 'regulated activity'.

Any adult (volunteering or employed) taking part in a 'regulated activity' must be checked. This includes roles that involve:

- contact with children and/or vulnerable adults and is of a 'specified nature' (this includes teaching, training, care, supervision, advice, treatment or transport); and takes place 'frequently' (i.e. once a month or more), 'intensively' (three or more days in a thirty-day period) or 'overnight';
- contact with children and/or vulnerable adults, is in a 'specified place' e.g. a school, and takes place 'frequently' or 'intensively';
- fostering and childcare;
- certain positions, e.g. school governor.

It is possible that the school's bursar or school secretary will be involved in collecting the paperwork in preparation for registration. It is beneficial to discuss this with them and/or the headteacher at an early stage of your work in schools.

Health and safety

In theory, each of your schools should make available to you their:

- Health and safety policy
- Child protection policy
- Lettings policy
- Staff handbook.

However, if you work with a large number of schools, being familiar with the full policies for each of these areas is not going to be practical. Instead, you might wish to note some important points for each school as a ready reference. Figure 7.1 shows some of the basic pieces of health and safety information you might need to collect.

	School 1	School 2	School 3
Recording of accidents – procedures			
Recording of faulty equipment – procedures			
Fire assembly point			
First aiders and first aid points			
Arrangements for entering the premises			
Visitor signing-in procedures			
Emergency contact numbers for key school staff			
Caretaker number in case of inclement weather			
Availability of induction information			
Other site security information			
Special lone working arrangements			
Lettings policy – particular points to note			

Figure 7.1 Health and safety ready reference

7.3 A list of useful websites on health and safety is provided in online resource 7.3 'Health and safety – further information'.

When liaising and working with agencies who might be working on the school premises out of hours, it is important that arrangements are in place to ensure:

- 7.4 they are aware of any specific requirements in the lettings policy (online resource 7.4 'Sample lettings policy')
- that providers have their own insurance
- 7.5 that each activity and each venue has a risk assessment (online resource 7.5 'Example risk assessment')
- appropriate vetting and barring arrangements are in place
- that providers have quick access to emergency contacts
- that schools have emergency contact details for providers
- there is awareness of signing in, security and fire precaution arrangements
- providers have received any induction information
- there is awareness of unlocking and locking procedures
- providers know what to do if there is an accident
- providers know what equipment they can use and procedures for using it
- there is understanding of any arrangements within the health and safety policy that are specific to out-of-hours provision
- 7.6 providers have first aid arrangements in place.

A useful checklist for clubs is available as online resource 7.6.

Equality and diversity

When implementing new activities and services it is important that you consider, within your professional capability, issues surrounding equality and diversity. The principles you might follow include:

- taking account of access arrangements to all facilities;
- the provision of a wide variety of activities that appeal to different groups within the community;
- consideration of the particular implications of religious beliefs and cultural considerations when arranging activities and services;
- ensuring that methods of communication take language needs into consideration;
- ensuring that you make every attempt to include the groups that might be more difficult to reach;
- consulting with and taking note of the needs of different community groups;
- seeking providers, activities and using resources from within the different community groups.

Issues to consider

The first issue to consider is which groups are represented in your community. This analysis of your catchment has already been covered in Chapter 4. However, Table 7.2 can help provide you with an overview of different groups and interests and the extent to which extended services in the cluster are catering for them.

When implementing new activities and services, it is important that you consider, within your professional capability, issues surrounding equality and diversity. You need to ensure that you are not discriminating and that you are offering equal opportunities to all in terms of access and range.

Issues to consider include:

- who is in the community (age ranges, ethnic groups, disabilities);
- restrictions on access (i.e. are there lifts to second floors, ramps);

- timings of the event (individuals who work, on benefits, attend religious events);
- accessibility of literature (i.e. translation, braille, easy to understand, pictures);
- food provided at events (is it appropriate to all cultures);
- cost of event (i.e. is this restrictive to some community members);
- providers (do you need specific requirements);
- advertising (i.e. is it inclusive or aimed at specific groups);
- transport to event (can all community members access the event).

Table 7.2 Core offer and the community

Community group	New arrivals
Childcare	Need to ensure that information is available in first languages and that advice is given about what is available and when
Menu of activities	Some temporary accommodation arrangements mean pupils have a long walk to school – need to consider signposting to more locally available clubs and activities
Parent support	Provide drop-in opportunities for parents to sit and chat and meet other parents Advice on housing benefits
Community access	Might benefit from providing some local facility for groups to arrange their own meetings or get-togethers
Adult and family learning	Need to provide language classes at accessible times (consider daytime and evening courses)

Categorization – school analysis

It can be difficult when filling in forms and funding applications to know what is the appropriate category to use. The following categories are those provided for ethnicity on RAISEonline material (a report which summarizes data for schools based on end of key stage assessment and tests and presents the information in different ways to help schools self-evaluate):

- British:
  - White
  - Irish
  - Traveller of Irish Heritage
  - Gypsy/ Roma
  - Any other white background
- Mixed:
  - White and black Caribbean
  - White and black African
  - White and Asian
  - Any other mixed background
- Asian or Asian British:
  - Indian
  - Pakistani
  - Bangladeshi
  - Any other Asian background
- Chinese
- Any other ethnic group.

These are the categories that school leaders use to analyse data to ensure that all groups are making the appropriate progress. It may be that following the school's analysis specific groups will be prioritized for intervention or for closer examination of what barriers there might be to their progress.

There is increasing emphasis by Ofsted on the performance of different groups within the school system. The ESC may find herself being increasingly involved in supporting schools in finding ways to engage particular groups in the catchment. This might include finding solutions or ideas for:

- supporting children who experience difficulties due to poor housing and living conditions;
- children and their families where language difficulties are a barrier;
- involving parents further in liaising with school where children have specific learning, behavioural or physical needs;
- encouraging parents to participate in adult learning programmes where this can help support difficulties their children are encountering;

- providing information for parents about intervention programmes in schools and additional support that might be being provided.

Top tips for keeping up with the practicalities

- Check that you have the information you need from your schools including who the designated person is and what the arrangements are for implementing vetting and barring arrangements.
- Never delay in reporting a child protection concern.
- The protection of the child is always the highest priority.
- Try to familiarize yourself and your providers with the basic health and safety requirements of your schools.
- Be clear about who is in your local community and how local provision appears for them.
- Be aware of ensuring equal access to activities and services.
- Try to involve all members of the community in making suggestions for activities and in identifying need.
- Don't underestimate the pivotal role you have in helping schools to deliver the duty for community cohesion – they need your help!

8 Applying for funding

Chapter aims

- To help you locate potential sources of funding
- To check the appropriateness of your source
- To present your project favourably

Topics

- Sources of funding
- Is it right for you?
- Presenting your project favourably

Figures

Tables

Online resources

- 8.1 Project management
- 8.2 Milestones
- 8.3 Budget sheet

Although we might think it should be otherwise, most ESCs will need to apply for funding for projects or even to support their own salary. Little is provided for free and in order to maximize the number of activities available, you will be involved in searching out resources both bidding for grants and seeking out 'in kind' arrangements.

Making applications can be time-consuming and can be pointless if you don't pitch right. Sourcing accurate information, checking its intended audience and producing the right evidence are essential aspects of a successful bid. This chapter intends to help you get it right first time and hopefully bring much needed resources to your community.

Sources of funding

You might want funding for several different purposes. For example:

- to start up a specific project that has been requested;
- for money to support the continuation of a project;
- for money to provide an additional facility as part of an existing project;
- for a specific item such as a minibus, computer or craft materials;
- for money to support existing or new staff.

The nature of your project will dictate the type of organization and funding sources you might apply to. Some funding sources will only consider supporting a new project with an aim that meets their own strict criteria. Others will only fund capital items and most are distrustful of anything connected to a school which they believe should be funded by the school budget.

Table 8.1 is a snapshot of those major organizations and funding sources that you might find useful to contact initially. It is likely that your local authority will have someone responsible for helping support schools who are looking for funding. They may well be aware of additional sources, some of them local and specific to the area. They may also be prepared to help you put together a bid.

Table 8.1 Funding sources

Organization or funding source	**Details**
Charitable trusts, grant making trusts or foundations	These are bodies that are set up, often by an individual, to invest money and then spend the income by offering funding, often for charitable activities. They are run by trustees, who decide how the money is given away. They offer funding to community and voluntary organizations and some will only give to those that have a charitable status. Some applications have to be sent by letter and some trustees only meet twice a year. It could take two or three months to receive a response. It varies between the trusts that you are applying to.
Charities	These are voluntary organizations that are set up for various purposes to perform activities that contribute to society.
Lottery distributors and public appeals	These include Big Lottery, Children in Need, Comic Relief and Sport Relief. They represent the very public and high-profile side of collections and donations.
Business support or corporate sponsorship	Local and national companies that might be willing to sponsor your project offer resources, facilities, services or a donation.
Local authority or borough council	The local authority or borough council may distribute grants or have awards that you can apply for.
Government funding (regional and central government)	These are statutory initiatives that come from the government departments.
European sources	European funding that is available for businesses and organizations.

Don't feel limited to applying to the larger sponsors and funds. These can be the most frequently approached and therefore the most selective. They can also be extremely stringent in terms of their expectations from the point of view both of a bid and of providing evidence about how it is spent. Sometimes smaller, local charities will look more favourably on your project – they are often exclusively aimed at projects within the vicinity. If you have a small, specific project it can be well worth seeking a local investor.

Is it right for you?

Before you take your bid too far, you need to ask some simple questions to check how appropriate it is for your purpose:

- Does the potential source only fund capital projects (buildings, large resources such as computers) or will it fund revenue (ongoing outlay such as staff salaries) too?
- Do you have to be a charity or will the potential source fund some school projects?
- Does the potential source have specific criteria that you will meet? For example, does it focus upon a particular catchment? Is it more sympathetic to particular groups, e.g. children with English as an Additional Language, children who are eligible for Free School Meals?
- What is the deadline for the application and when will it be considered? Does this fit in with your own time frame?
- How detailed is the application? Is it something you have the capacity to complete at this time?
- What will be the level of project evaluation expected if you are successful – is this something you can cope with?
- Do you need to demonstrate that you have consulted about the project?
- Is it necessary to have the involvement of a community partnership and or a multi-agency working group?
- Might a community partnership be able to help you with it? (See section 'Working in partnership and management' page 121.)

There is no point in getting half way through an application to suddenly realize that you don't meet all the criteria or that the deadline is next week.

Other factors that you may need to consider well in advance include:

- Do you need references? If so, you should ask well in advance and make sure the potential source is clear about what your project is and what will be expected from the source.
- Do you have the statistical information you need? A lot of forms will require information about how many children the project will help. It can be beneficial to have a breakdown to hand of ethnicity, FSM and SEN from your schools.
- Does the potential source need accounts to be attached or a detailed budget break down? If so, you may need to involve a school bursar – they will need to know well in advance.

Presenting your project favourably

It might be obvious but you need to be absolutely clear what you are asking for. It is beneficial when considering a new project to map it under project management headings. This will not only enable you to describe your project succinctly at a later date but will prompt you to consider who else might help you with it and if there is anything else you need to research.

Figure 8.1 identifies the columns and their headings that should help you to identify the main aspects of your project. It is also available as online resource 8.1. 8.1

Aims	What is the aim of the project?	
Evidence	How do you know it is needed?	
Benefits (outcomes)	What are the benefits to the participants?	
Activities	What activities will you deliver?	
Resources	What resources do you require?	
Providers	Who can help you to deliver the project?	
Roles	What will you and partners do to deliver the project?	
Evaluation	How will you know you have achieved your outcomes?	

Figure 8.1 Project management

You need to do your homework. You will need to be clear about what the need is, who will benefit from it and what difference you expect your project to make.

Aims

You need to be clear about what you are trying to achieve from your project. Aims need to be overarching and show high expectations without being over ambitious. It could be beneficial to link them to the Every Child Matters Outcomes:

- be healthy
- stay safe
- enjoy and achieve
- make a positive contribution
- achieve economic well-being.

So, for example, a project requesting a bike shed might use 'to help children in the local area achieve the ECM outcome of being healthy'. You might want to explain this further by adding 'by encouraging children to cycle to school and increase their levels of activity'.

Evidence

You must to be able to demonstrate that there is a need for the project you are proposing. Ideally, this need will have come from your target group of people and you will be able to show the evidence for this. So, for example, 'following a survey of parents 30 per cent said they would like to attend a behaviour management course' or 'the mother and toddler group has requested the use of an empty classroom for their meetings in which they can also receive advice and support from other agencies'.

Ideally you would also be able to demonstrate that of that 30 per cent some of the families were struggling with examples of challenging behaviour and in x number of cases there had been fixed-term exclusions. You could set out your evidence as in Table 8.2.

Table 8.2 Identifying need

Target group	**Need**	**Need identified through**	**Evidence for this**
Parents with challenging children in danger of exclusion	Behaviour management course	Parent survey	30% of parents requested behaviour management classes in the survey Two of those responding have children at risk of fixed-term exclusion
Single mothers with children under three years old	Facilities to meet with one another and receive external support	Mother and toddler group request following annual meeting	Ten families currently attending – three of these are single-parent families who have been subject to a CAF

The more information you can collect to increase your evidence base, the better. So, for example, you might add that of the 30 per cent of parents requesting the course, all were living in temporary accommodation, or of the mother and toddler group that another three families were also on the Free School Meals register.

You can increase your evidence base by calling together the target group and discussing their needs with them. This can provide you with more specific information that can be impressive for those on bidding panels. Therefore, you could document that parents are struggling to maintain discipline at home as well as their children being in trouble at school and that it is not only the course that will be beneficial but the opportunity for parents in similar situations to meet together and discuss their problems.

You need to keep in mind that funding bids for teenagers will need to be led by the young people themselves. You can help steer and support them but it will be expected that the drive for the provision comes from them.

Benefits

What difference will this project make to those participating? You will need to consider what the outcomes will be and how you will measure these. It is insufficient to assume that something just taking place or people attending is a sufficient indicator that the project is worthwhile.

Indicators will help you to measure the difference you are making. These are the steps the participants are taking towards the outcome. You will need to consider how you might measure progress against the indicators. Table 8.3 provides some examples of outcomes and indicators.

Table 8.3 Outcomes and indicators

Outcome	**Activity**	**Indicator**	**Means of measurement**
The improved behaviour management skills of targeted parents	Behaviour management course for parents	80% of those attending report improved behaviour of their children at home	Participants' survey at the end of the course
Single-parents feel more confident in their child-rearing skills and are able to ask for and implement support	Mother and toddler group situated on school site with external support available	Families are no longer in need of a CAF as identified by the professionals attending	CAF meeting minutes and report from key worker

You might be able to identify 'steps' that represent taking starting need to intended outcome. For example, it is a very big jump for a family currently in need of a Common Assessment Framework to not needing one. It is beneficial to break this down into steps – at least for your own use – as shown in Figure 8.2.

Parents are isolated and struggling to cope

↓

Parents are sharing their worries and difficulties

↓

Parents are listening to advice and acting upon it

↓

There is evidence that there are changes in the parents' ability to cope

↓

Parents are coping better and asking for additional support

↓

Professionals and the key worker feel the parents are now able to continue without the CAF using the current support network

Figure 8.2 Steps along the way

Your means of measurement will often consist of a questionnaire or survey of some kind. It is beneficial if you use the same kind of questions before the activity begins and after it finishes. This will help you to monitor the amount of progress that has been made. However, questionnaires are not the only way you can collect evidence of progress. You can also use observations, focus groups, plenary sessions, interviews, discussions, administrative records, local area statistics, audio recordings and transcripts as your tools.

Activities

The activities and services that you will provide to achieve your aims are the real 'meat' in your planning. However, they do not just materialize over night and the stark statement 'behaviour management course for parents' is the cover for a whole series of actions and their 'milestones' that you must implement first.

8.2

As shown in Figure 8.3 (template available as online resource 8.2), it can be beneficial to set out the actions that will lead to the activity being in place and how you can keep check that your plans are in order.

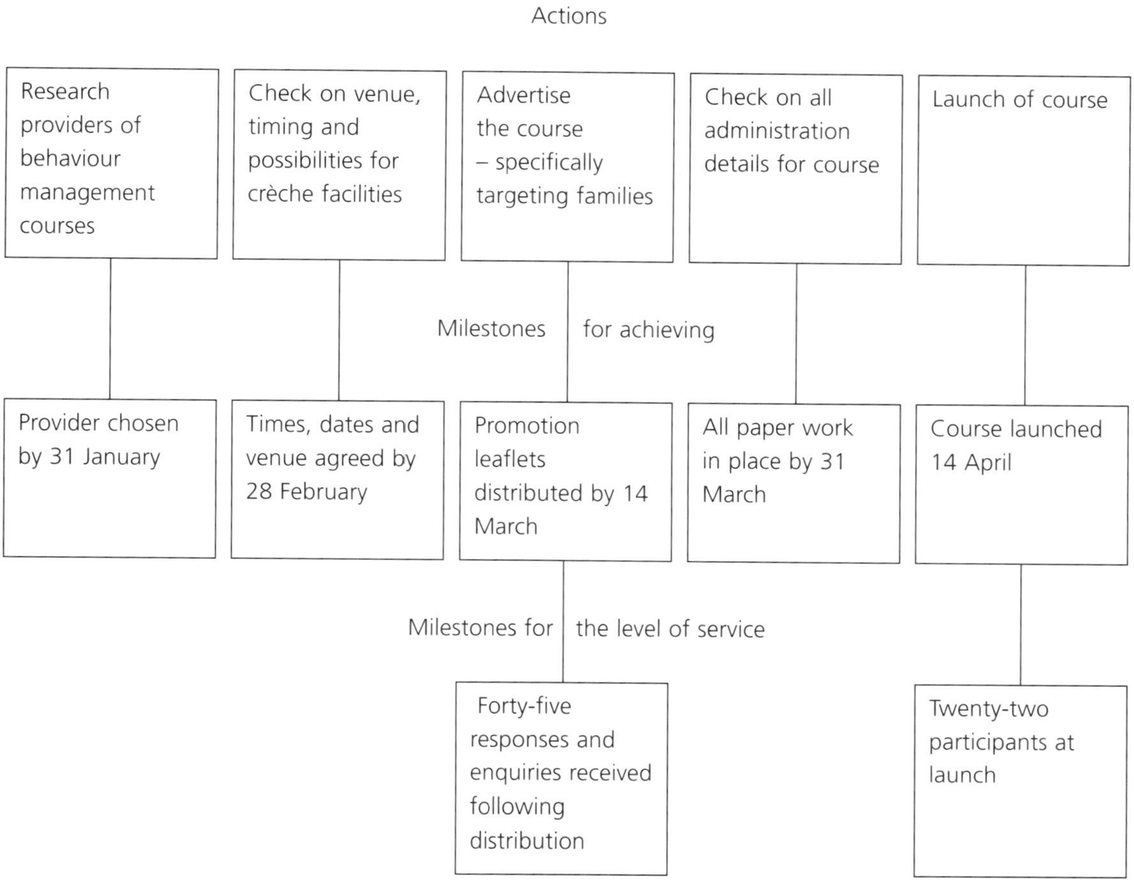

Figure 8.3 Milestones

Resources and budget

It is important to be realistic when planning your budget and obtain approximate costs from source if at all possible. For some applications you will need to include a budget spreadsheet that identifies precise costs (example given in online resource 8.3). You may need to seek help for this from a school bursar or local authority finance departments. 8.3

Keep copies of your quotations, as the funding stream may ask to see this information. It is advisable to gather three competitive quotes before deciding which you should take. This demonstrates that you are seeking best value for the purchases you make.

Think carefully about the additional costs that might surround your provision. For example:

- Will you be required to pay the school caretaker for opening/closing the school building?
- Will you be expected to contribute towards heating/lighting costs?
- Will there be a charge for cleaning?
- Will you need to pay someone to audit your accounts?
- Will you need to buy basic resources such as stamps, paper, envelopes?
- What will the cost of refreshments be (if any)?
- If you are employing someone, what will the on costs be?
- What will be the cost of recruitment (including advertising)?

Much will depend upon the willingness of your venue to support and contribute. If you are lucky, there may be match funding available or the school may be prepared to fundraise to support the project. They may also be prepared to waver any additional premises costs and/or contribute the time of a bursar to help you manage your accounts.

At the planning stage, your bid will be an estimate and it can be expected that there will be changes to cost over time. You should slightly over estimate the cost including some allowance for inflation, being aware that in most cases any under spend will need to be returned. This is better than finding half way through your project that the money available has dried up.

Many donating organizations are very specific about whether they will only donate to capital projects or if they will pay for staff salaries. If a salary is involved, you may need to demonstrate that you have given consideration to how the project might continue once this funding source is finished. Providers are keen to see that there is an element of sustainability in what you do and you may need to argue the case for this.

You may also need to convince your potential fund that the project is not something that is statutory and should be provided by the school. Understandably there is often a great deal of hesitancy in funding something that is school-based.

The natural question is 'shouldn't the school's budget be paying for this'? For this reason it is an advantage to identify local partners who might be prepared to take the lead on the project.

Working in partnership

You cannot implement all the necessary projects yourself. You should be looking at every opportunity for agencies and organizations that you can work with and that will take some of the responsibility for running and organizing projects from you. You might consider:

- Are there any community or voluntary organizations that might be interested in organizing the project?
- Do any local groups have the particular strengths or expertise to act as providers within the project?
- Could you use the PTA or 'Friends of…' to apply for funding?

The most beneficial approach might be to create a purpose-built group whose role is to apply for funding for projects. This would need to be a voluntary management committee community group with no more than one member from the school. In addition, you would need individuals from the area including services and community members. You would need to establish the committee officially with a constitution, secretary, chair and a bank account. However, it could be worth it in the long run if they were able to take the burdensome role from you of applying for funding.

Whoever takes the lead, someone will need to sign the application form and be responsible for the bid. Be clear at the outset who this is and that they understand the amount of work which might be involved.

And finally…

Before you send your application:

- take a copy of the form

- make a record of when you sent it and also record any further communications you have with the funding body
- make sure that you have included any supplementary information requested and have signed and dated the form.

Then you wait. And hope that after all that effort you are successful.

Reference sources for funding

The following sources of information might be useful.

For preparing funding bids:

Burns, S. and MacKeith, J. (2006) *Explaining the Difference Your Project Makes. A BIG Guide to Using an Outcomes Approach.* BIG Lottery Fund

Smyth, J. (2005) *The Guide to UK Company Giving*. London: DSC

For lists of funding sources:

Routledge, K. (2005) *Fundraising Guidance: Study Support/Out of Schools Hours Learning* (oshl). Coventry: ContinYou

Schools etc. magazine produced by ContinYou

For putting together your evidence and evaluation:

Aimhigher West Yorkshire (c. 2008) *Evaluation Toolkit: Easy Steps to Evaluate: A Guide for Practitioners.* West Yorkshire: Aim Higher

DfES (2005b) *Evidence and Evaluation*. Available from:

www.teachernet.gov.uk/docbank/index.cfm?id=8290 (accessed 16 February 2009)

Field, J. (2003) *Evaluating Community Projects*. Leicester: NIACE.

9 Engaging with parents and carers

Chapter aims

- To provide suggestions for ways of engaging parents
- To help you identify ways of working with carers and looked-after children
- To help you identify ways of engaging hard-to-reach parents
- To help you engage parents in adult learning

Topics

- Ideas for engaging parents
- Carers and looked-after children
- Hard-to-reach parents
- Adult learning

Figure

- 9.1 Engaging parents

Tables

- 9.1 Strategies for engagement

Effective working relationships with parents and carers are absolutely essential for schools. Of course, it was not always considered important. For hundreds of years, parents were kept well away from the school building and what went on within was considered to be none of their business. Be aware – some people still hold this view! However, in today's climate of ECM and extended schools there is no room for this approach. The reasons are simple:

- Children spend the majority of time within their family circle.
- The most formative years in child development are before the majority of children enter formal education.
- The conditions experienced within the home environment have a long-lasting, profound and continuous impact upon the well-being of children.
- The attitudes, experiences and expectations of family have a very significant impact upon that of the child.

Although this chapter is entitled 'Parents and carers', the wider family group also comes under this category. For some children grandparents are the main carers and within the extended family they spend significant time with aunts, uncles and other relatives. Re-formed families are a major part of our society today. Many children will have step-parents and siblings. Special weekend arrangements might exist and children may be adept at moving from one family unit to another. Or not. This chapter uses the term 'parents' throughout to mean those who have the closest, most frequent and nurturing contact with children, in whatever form that might be. Your role as ESC will need to embrace the full range of carers that support the children in your different schools.

Ideas for engaging parents

Parents are the community group most likely to benefit from the additional facilities, activities and services you enable. You have a constant channel for communication through their children and a captive audience in parents' evening queues. However, there will be some parents who seem to attend everything and some who you will never see. It is likely that those who are most reluctant to participate are actually the ones who have most need of the services on offer.

However, you will also have some parents who fall somewhere in the middle. They may have a history of keeping a distance from school, simply because times of access are not convenient or they've been through it all before. It is this group of parents who might be engaged with a little persuasion and perhaps here is where you might start first.

Parents can be put off by formal attempts to engage them. Announcing a meeting to discuss parental engagement is unlikely to bring them in. Instead you might try:

- spending time chatting to parents on the playground – talk to them about the services on offer and ask them for their views;
- piggybacking another event e.g. careers day, parents' evening, open day;
- running a coffee morning for parents;
- arranging a community event in another venue rather than the school;
- children performing at an event so that parents will come and watch them;
- children producing the invitations;
- offering free food or nibbles;
- holding events at different times to make them more accessible to those who work;
- having a themed event to encourage general interest;
- running one-off information events e.g. dealing with headlice, drugs awareness – parents can come for information without have to commit themselves regularly;
- running parenting courses which will allow parents the opportunity to engage with the school and meet other parents;
- producing a newsletter for parents or putting information in the school newsletter to keep them informed;
- offering support for parents in relation to curriculum areas e.g. helping with maths homework, so that they can help their children;

- finding out what your parents are good at and encouraging them to help out or run activities;
- producing a calendar or diary of school events for every parent, so they are informed in advance.

Making sure your plans run smoothly

Imagine the scene. You have spent days encouraging a few reluctant parents to attend your event. You have arranged the course provider and have even found someone to run the crèche. You arrive at the school in good time but only to discover that the room you thought you might use is being occupied by the peripatetic woodwind lesson. Disaster. It can happen to everyone, but there are ways of trying to avoid it happening at all.

Top tips to make your parent events run smoothly

- Check well ahead of the event which rooms are available, book them and then check again a week before hand just to make sure.
- Make sure that the school receptionist is aware that parents are coming to an event and knows where to send them when they arrive.
- Organize refreshments – you might need to try to persuade someone to help you with this.
- Spend time finding out what times are convenient for your parents.
- Try to make sure that your event doesn't clash with something else, such as an important football match or another school's annual gala.
- Use every means of advertising the event at your disposal.
- Keep to the advertised times. Try not to delay the start whilst waiting for others and make sure you finish on time.
- If possible, provide parents with something to take away with them, perhaps a summary of what has been discussed or a 'where to find out more' sheet.

- Consider the layout of your room carefully – are the chairs too small to be comfortable?
- What resources are needed? Don't disappear during the event to find a flipchart.
- Check with the school which toilet facilities they would like you to use.
- Discuss any arrangements as necessary with the school caretaker.

In the end you cannot remove every eventuality, but the more you have thought ahead and prepared the more likely it is to be a success. Once you have involved parents successfully, there is a greater chance that they will come more willingly to anything you arrange in future.

Be conscious of issues to do with confidentiality at your events. Parent politics and tensions with members of school staff will always exist. You should try not to become involved in any complaints or rising issues. Where difficulties are mentioned, you should refer parents to the proper methods of communication. A key benefit of your role is that you are not directly a member of school staff and as such your degree of impartiality should be treasured. There may be occasions when you need to speak to a member of staff about something that has been raised. However, wherever possible the individual parent should be encouraged to discuss issues directly and not through you. You are not a go-between and becoming involved as such could get in the way of the core function of your role.

Involving parents – different angles

Schools provide many opportunities for parents to be involved. Schools will appreciate it if you can help them recruit willing volunteers and equally these links can help you develop other services. Parents can be involved through:

- *Parent governors*. Depending upon your catchment, it can be extremely difficult to recruit parent governors. Having parents on the governing body who have an interest and involvement in the extended schools agenda can be greatly beneficial.

- *Adult volunteers*. Schools benefit from having a willing team of volunteers who can accompany school trips, back books, listen to readers, help organize the library. This kind of involvement is not just beneficial for the school but can also provide parents wishing to return to work with the necessary experience for their CV. It can build parental self-esteem and provide them with insight into the way that school works.
- *Parent/ teacher and 'Friends of…'*. PTAs and Friends groups are an essential fundraising body for many schools. They also provide parents with social events and activities and can enable parent to network. It is important to encourage a representative group of parents on these bodies.

Carers and looked-after children

A looked-after child is provided for by the local authority and may be placed with foster carers, a member of the extended family or in a residential home. Care can either be temporary or permanent as a result of a voluntary agreement by their parents or as a result of a care order.

There has been a lot of attention given to looked-after children because of their particularly low levels of attainment. Children in care are five times less likely to achieve five good GCSEs, nine times more likely to be excluded from school and six times less likely to enter higher education than their peers. In order to address these differences for looked-after children, legislation now requires that looked-after children:

- are given the highest priority in school admission arrangements;
- do not have their education disrupted if at all possible because of changing placements;
- are allocated a designated teacher;
- receive personalized learning.

Schools are expected to monitor the progress of looked-after children carefully and implement strategies to address any identified needs they may have. Schools may wish to draw attention to the looked-after children in the school and target them and their carers for support.

As such, you might beneficially monitor the activities that children are involved in and target carers specifically where family learning opportunities arise. However, it is also important to note that looked-after children are keen to be treated in the same way as their peers and do not want to be singled out for additional attention.

Some foster carers may experience difficulties because of travel distance from the school and other commitments they might have. It is beneficial if possible for time to be taken at least annually to discuss with families how they might be supported in accessing extended schools provision. Where this is difficult for the ESC, the discussion could be held between the designated teacher and foster carers.

Hard-to-reach parents

Parents may be reluctant to engage with a school for many different reasons. Their own experiences of school may have been difficult and they may have preconceptions about what to expect. In some cases a family may have difficult relationships with all institutions and authority-type figures. They may see school as another example of a public body which is disinterested in their needs. Language difficulties, working shifts, frequent moves and poor living conditions can all affect a family's willingness and/or ability to engage.

Even though parents are difficult to reach, this does not mean that they are any the less interested in the progress of their children. Every attempt should be made to find some way of encouraging and enabling parents to take a full part in the extended services agenda. In order to do this, you must be creative and try different approaches. Try using the Figure 9.1 to develop an understanding of your parents who stay away and the strategies that might be used to help engage them. Of course, in some cases some parents are just too busy or do not need the services you offer. In the end, they have the right not to engage if they prefer not to.

Figure 9.1 Engaging parents

Starting from the questions on the left, use the spaces under 'aim' and 'strategy' to identify a focus for your support and a means to apply it. Table 9.1 identifies some of the strategies that might be tried depending upon the type of engagement you are looking for and the reason you have established for them being hard to reach.

Table 9.1 Strategies for engagement

Issue	Strategy
Practical difficulties	• Try arranging groups/support at different times • Use different methods of communication e.g. email • Arrange for translations of written communication • Organize childcare and crèches
Don't see the need	• Target families at the point of transition • Focus on identifying the particular needs/benefits for the child and family • Write to parents inviting them individually and explaining why • Involve other parents in promoting the benefits
History of family non-engagement	• Involve the child in encouraging family to attend • Arrange forums appropriate to specific groups • Use word of mouth – through any friends who are engaged • Make activities/events informal and as low key as possible • Consider using other local venues for meetings/activities

In many cases it can be a very slow process. Generations of a family can have a deep distrust of schools and this will not be reversed over night. Some general approaches that can help include:

- *The parents' room*. Having a dedicated space for parents to congregate is beneficial. Ideally this might be a room, however, even part of a corridor with a few chairs, a noticeboard, some toys for younger children and information leaflets can demonstrate to parents that they are welcome.

- *Signage*. It is beneficial to look around the school from the point of view of a new parent or a parent who does not speak English as a first language. Are signs to the entrance and reception clear? Are signs also provided in community languages? The type and quality of signs provides clear messages to the community.

- *Through the children*. The involvement of children can be a powerful lever in bringing parents in to school. Where children are performing or if they have contributed in some way through writing invitations, painting pictures or providing resources or ideas, there is more likelihood that parents will follow. Curriculum evenings where children do demonstrations, support sessions arranged after a class assembly, coffee mornings on sports days are approaches that can help hook parents in.

- *Away from school.* An ESC is in a strong position to be able to find an alternative local venue that parents might find less intimidating than school. Often nurseries and children's centres will provide a more comfortable environment that parents might already be familiar with.

- *We need you.* Sometimes parents will respond more positively when their involvement is requested as a contributor. We can all find ourselves defensive when it is suggested that there is something we need or are lacking in. This kind of reaction can be overcome if the initial contacts aim to involve parents in actively helping the school. Once a relationship has been developed then opportunities can emerge for raising discussions about more sensitive areas.

- *Use your contacts.* Disengagement is a deep-rooted problem. It is important to talk to members of staff who have experience of the family and the children in order to ascertain where the disengagement originates and what their views on it might be. If you are responsible for several schools, you are not in a position to work with all these families on an individual basis. However, discussions with other members of staff can help you develop more generic methods and strategies for working with groups of families.

Adult learning

If you are running adult learning, family learning or fun recreational activities, there are some issues to consider when aiming to engage parents and, more importantly, attempting to maintain their interest.

- Offer family learning activities, as parents will be encouraged to come to learn with their child.

- Start by offering some tasters or fun courses and advertise the activities as fun.

- If you are running courses, such as adult learning or family learning, encourage them to come along to try it out the first week and don't tell them it's a ten-week course!

- If the course has an optional exam or assessment attached (i.e. Literacy or Numeracy), do not mention this at the beginning of the course.

- Ensure that the furniture in the room is appropriate for adult learners, including chairs and tables.
- If the course is at the school and out of hours, make sure you meet the parents to direct them, or put up signs.
- Run courses at a community venue, such as a children's centre, which will not have barriers to attending for parents with unpleasant past experiences of schools.
- Work with the school to determine if some programmes are best run as discrete provision (i.e. handling teenage behaviour), depending on the parents.
- If space allows, the school could adapt an area to become a 'parents' room' or be designated for community use, so it feels more welcoming to the community and owned by them.

10 Ofsted inspection

Chapter aims

- To summarize the inspection process
- To explain what the Self-Evaluation Form is and how you might be involved
- To identify what your role might be during an inspection
- To consider how you might help your school and childcare facilities prepare

Topics

- Ofsted inspection
- The Self-Evaluation Form
- Your role during the inspection

Figure

- 10.1 Health check

Tables

- 10.1 SEF headings
- 10.2 Community cohesion
- 10.3 Focus for inspectors
- 10.4 Barriers to learning

Online resources

- 10.1 Preparation for inspection crib sheet (worked example)
- 10.2 Health check

No one working within the school community can be immune from the impact of Ofsted on the school and its environment. Most school staff, particularly the leadership team, live in fear of it and no matter how it is 'sold' the fact remains that careers are launched and sunk on the basis of the judgement.

The level of accountability that the system currently promotes and its overall name and shame approach means that every provider within and around school needs to be aware of his/her potential role during inspection and how the provision offered is covered within the schedule.

Extended services have gradually come to be more of a feature of the inspection. With the duty to promote community cohesion, it is likely that you will already have been quizzed about what aspects of your work could fall under this heading. In fact, here you have a powerful lever. Any provision that you consider important to establish has a good chance of success if it can be demonstrated that it supports community cohesion.

This never-ending, constantly evolving inspection regime changed again in September 2009. The advice and information given here is written on the basis of what is currently available and it is important that you confirm with your school if there have been any further updates before committing too much time and energy to the schedule.

The documents used to compile this advice include:

- 'Using the early years evaluation schedule' Ofsted (August 2008)
- 'Conducting the inspection' Ofsted (February 2009)
- 'Ofsted's evaluation of the autumn term 2008 pilot inspections of maintained schools' Ofsted (April 2009)
- The draft of the new SEF available from www.ofsted.gov.uk/Ofsted-home/Forms-and-guidance.

Ofsted inspection

Currently there is a three-year cycle for the inspection of schools with normally two days' notice and usually taking two days to complete. However, plans to inspect those schools judged to be good or outstanding every six years were put in place from September 2009. These schools would, however, experience a health check during the interim years.

The Lead Inspector (LI) contacts the school prior to the inspection to decide on the format of the inspection over the two days. The LI prepares a pre-inspection briefing which describes the extent to which the school's view of itself, taken from the Self-Evaluation Form (SEF), is borne out by available evidence.

During the inspection inspectors will be involved in:

- observing lessons;
- observing behaviour at breaktimes and between lessons;
- talking to staff, pupils and others where appropriate;
- checking evidence form written sources;
- gathering evidence about current standards.

The first day is usually spent observing teachers teach and meeting with members of the senior leadership team and governors. The second day the inspection usually finishes at lunchtime with inspectors writing their report in the afternoon. There is then a feedback session for the senior leadership team and the chair of governors.

Parents' views are currently collected through a questionnaire and parents and carers can also ask to speak with an inspector. Pupils are asked about:

- the extent to which the school seeks and acts upon their views;
- how the school improves behaviour;
- how the school handles bullying;
- how the school promotes racial equality;
- what the strengths of the school are;

- whether they feel safe;
- what they do if they are troubled.

After the inspection, the report is finalized and a letter is drafted to learners. Schools receive electronic versions of the report within three weeks of the end of the inspection and they are allowed five days to distribute the report to parents and the letter to learners. Following this the report appears on the internet.

There are four possible grades: outstanding, good, satisfactory or inadequate. If a school is judged to be inadequate, they are either placed in special measures or are given a notice to improve. Following this there are return visits from Her Majesty's Inspectors to report on the progress of the school against its key areas for improvement.

Inspecting childcare on school premises

From September 2008 Ofsted inspectors have been making judgements for all providers working with children from birth to five years. This includes provision from nurseries to out-of-school clubs and from childminders. Where there is childcare on the school premises they will be inspected separately. However, the inspection will usually take place at around the same time as the main school inspection.

The Self-Evaluation Form

The Self-Evaluation Form (SEF) is an online document that schools produce in preparation for inspection. It provides opportunity for the school to demonstrate that they are able to self-evaluate their provision and demonstrate the capacity to act on the results. Prior to completion of the SEF it is expected that schools will:

- consult with stakeholders
- analyse data
- monitor standards of teaching and learning

- track the progress of different groups across the school
- demonstrate a clear link from self-evaluation to school improvement planning
- demonstrate the ability to be self-critical.

The overall emphasis of the SEF is upon standards of attainment, the ECM outcomes and pupil well-being. Recently added has been the duty to promote community cohesion.

SEFs are generally completed by the senior leadership team. However, there are parts of the current and proposed form that have a particular relevance to you. Some schools may even ask you to contribute. If they don't, it is still likely that they will include reference to provision that you organize. The headings in Table 10.1 are taken from the new-style SEF which was implemented in September 2009. The headings of most relevance to your role are in italic.

Table 10.1 SEF headings

Outcomes: how well are pupils doing, taking account of any variation?
A2.1 Pupils' attainment
A2.2 The quality of pupils' learning and their progress
A2.3 The quality of learning for pupils with special educational needs and/or disabilities and their progress
A2.4 Pupils' achievement and the extent to which they enjoy their learning
A2.5 The extent to which pupils feel safe
A2.6 Pupils' behaviour
A2.7 The extent to which pupils adopt healthy lifestyles
A2.8 The extent to which pupils contribute to the school and wider community
A2.9 Pupils' attendance
A2.10 The extent to which pupils develop workplace and other skills that will contribute to their future economic well-being
A2.11 The extent of pupils' spiritual, moral, social and culutral development

Table 10.1 SEF headings *continued*

How effective is the provision?
A3.1 The quality of teaching
A3.2 The use of assessment to support learning
A3.3 The extent to which the curriculum meets pupils' needs, including, where relevant, through partnerships
A3.4 The effectiveness of care, guidance and support
How effective are leadership and management?
A.4.1 The effectiveness of leadership and management in embedding ambition and driving improvement
A4.2 The leadership and management of teaching and learning
A4.3 The effectiveness of the governing body in challenging and supporting the school so that weaknesses are tackled decisively and statutory responsibilities met
A4.4 The effectiveness of the school's engagement with parents and carers
A4.5 The effectiveness of partnerships in promoting learning and well-being
A4.6 The effectiveness with which the school promotes equal opportunity and tackles discrimination
A4.7 The effectiveness of safeguarding procedures
A4.8 The effectiveness with which the school promotes community cohesion
A4.9 The effectiveness with which the school deploys resources to achieve value for money

Although it might be argued that the provision of extended services has an impact on many more, if not all, of these sections, the ones in italic have the most obvious implication for you.

If you are asked to contribute it is important to:

- be as succinct as you can
- avoid pure description
- include what the benefits and outcomes of the prcvision have been.

Your role during the inspection

For many parts of the inspection you will have limited, if any, involvement. Where the focus is upon teaching and learning, although you may have supported schools in identifying barriers and looking for ways of overcoming them, you are unlikely to be directly involved.

Your greatest contributions are likely to be in relation to:

- the inspection of the school's duty to promote community cohesion;
- the support provided for groups of students who are facing barriers to learning;
- the involvement of parents and carers;
- the effect of partnership work.

10.1 You might use the online resource 10.1 'Preparation for inspection crib sheet' to remind staff about the extended services that the school does provide. A folder for your school containing different information and evidence surrounding extended services may be appreciated by Ofsted. You might include:

- information sent to governors
- cluster newsletters
- the core offer at the school
- examples of signposting
- examples of projects
- case studies

- community access
- case studies of multi-agency work
- case studies of community cohesion.

Community cohesion

The duty to promote community cohesion is perhaps the aspect of the inspection schedule which is most related to your work.

The Education Act 2002 states that:

> The governing body of a maintained school shall, in discharging their functions relating to the conduct of the school –
> (a) promote the well-being of pupils at the school, and
> (b) in the case of a school in England, promote community cohesion.

The duty came into effect from 1 September 2007 and inspection of this duty began in September 2008.

There are four dimensions of community cohesion as shown in Table 10.2.

Table 10.2 Community cohesion

Dimension	Details
The school community	The schools and its pupils, parents, carers and families. The school staff, governors and community users of the school's facilities
The community within which the school is located	The school's geographical community – people living and working in that area. It includes the immediate neighbourhood and the city or local authority area that the school is in
The UK community	All schools within the UK
The global community	The EU and the rest of the world

So what will inspectors be looking for?

Table 10.3 Focus for inspectors

Focus for the inspectors	What will it tell them?	Evidence the inspectors will collect
The views of pupils and their knowledge and understanding	How the school's actions and ethos are having an effect upon the pupils and how well the school is promoting good relationships and mutual understanding	They will ask pupils about their community and the way the school is involved in it – testing out what's claimed in the SEF They will ask pupils how they get on with each other in the school and how they are encouraged to work together by the school
Quality of provision	How the curriculum and teaching reflect the diversity of the school community	They will be looking to see how schemes of work provide a global and international perspective as well as reflecting the cultures of significant groups within the school What aspects of the curriculum are helping pupils to understand one another and different nationalities, religions and cultures
Promotion of equity and excellence	How the school reflects its catchment	Representation of different groups on the governing body Representation of different groups on the staff Links made with representatives of different significant groups Consideration of how information and school events can be made accessible to different groups
Level of engagement of its pupils	How involved different groups of children are within the school	Details about groups or individuals attending extra-curricular clubs Are any groups overly represented in exclusions? Evidence of strategies used
Self-evaluation and awareness	How effective the school is in identifying what needs to be done to promote community cohesion and what the needs of its community are	Is there evidence of different groups being consulted? Have their views been acted upon? Evidence of school priorities including the development of community cohesion?

In order to ensure that inspectors recognize the extent to which your schools are promoting community cohesion, you might want to draw their attention to:

- the school's awareness of the needs of different ethnic, religious, non-religious and socio-economic groups;
- how you have identified the needs of parents and community groups;
- the fact that actions for the groups identified link in with the needs of the school (this might link with the School Improvement Planning Framework);
- how the school is providing for the different groups through representation within the school, consultation processes, involvement in extended services provision;
- the extent to which the school has tried to engage with different groups of parents;
- the extent to which the school has linked with other schools with a contrasting pupil population;
- the extent to which extra-curricular activities reflect diversity within the school community.

Details of the number of children using different activities and a breakdown of these according to gender, ethnicity and socio-economic status can be very useful. In fact it will be expected that you are tracking the uptake of activities and putting measures in place to address any in balances or difficulties with access.

Figure 10.1 might be used by yourself in conjunction with the senior leadership as a health check prior to inspection (also available as online resource 10.2). 10.2

Example of promoting community cohesion	Level of provision	Evidence
The school has developed links with other schools as part of partnership arrangements		
The school has made international links and these are grounded in the curriculum		
Pupils work together cooperatively on joint projects within the school and between schools		
Teachers and governing bodies benefit from links with different schools – broadening their experiences by working with different groups of pupils, teachers and governors		
The school shares its facilities with the local community and with other schools		
Meaningful intercultural activities are organized such as sport, drama, music, festivals, volunteering activities and school trips		
The school works together with community representatives – some of who come into school to work with pupils or to lead assemblies		
Pupils are encouraged to make a positive contribution in the local area		
The pupil voice is prominent within the school and is acted upon		
Pupils are encouraged to take responsibility and to evaluate how well the school is building community cohesion		
The school maintains strong links with other agencies such as the youth support service, the police, different religious groups, social care and health professionals		
Links are developed with work placed learning providers and other employers		
Pupils are placed in voluntary community based activities		
There is engagement with parents through curriculum evenings, parent and child courses, family liaison work		
The school makes every effort to engage its hard-to-reach parents		

Figure 10.1 Health check

Inspecting maintained schools' duty to promote community cohesion: guidance for inspectors

The document 'Inspecting maintained schools' duty to promote community cohesion: guidance for inspectors' (Ofsted, 2008) includes pointers for schools and their staff. According to this guidance examples of delivering community cohesion within the scope of the ESC include:

- assemblies involve members of the local and wider communities;
- the school is welcoming to all sections of the community;
- the school has developed links with other schools as part of partnership arrangements;
- pupils work together collaboratively on joint projects within the school and between schools;
- teachers and governors benefit from links with different schools – broadening their experiences by working with different groups of pupils, teachers and governors;
- the school shares its facilities with the local community and with other schools;
- meaningful intercultural activities are organized such as sport, drama, music, festivals, volunteering activities and school trips;
- the school works together with community representatives – some of who come into school to work with pupils or to lead assemblies;
- pupils are encouraged to make a positive contribution in the local area;
- the pupil voice is prominent within the school and is acted upon;
- the school maintains strong links with other agencies such as the youth support service, the police, different religious groups, social care and health professionals;
- pupils are placed in voluntary community based activities;
- there is engagement with parents through curriculum evenings, parent and child courses, family liaison work;
- ways of engaging the hard-to-reach parents have been developed.

Barriers to learning

It will be expected that your school is closely monitoring the progress of all pupils, particularly those more at risk of failure. This will then lead to discussions about why some pupils or groups of pupils are not making the progress they should and what might be done about it.

The barriers to learning or 'blockers' might be aspects of the standards agenda that you and the services you promote become involved with. For example, the 'School Improvement Planning Framework' (TDA, 2008) refers to 'lack of parental expectations' and 'being a carer' as potential blockers to successful learning. You might be asked to support the school in collecting the evidence to show what the school has done to address these 'blockers'. Some examples are given in Table 10.4.

Table 10.4 Barriers to learning

Pupils/ groups not making sufficient progress	**Identified barriers to learning**	**Recommended strategies to try**	**Follow-on actions**
Child A Child B Child C (all subjects)	Poor behaviour from all the children in the family resulting in time out of class	Behaviour management course for parents Involvement of school behaviour support service (BSS)	Behaviour management course to start in June BSS to meet with deputy headteacher to discuss next steps
Year 3 (maths)	Poor retention of mental maths facts and times tables	Workshop for parents to help raise awareness of how they might help	Two evenings arranged for May

Involvement of parents/carers

A large amount of the work that you do involves parents and carers. In terms of evidence it should be sufficient to show inspectors (if asked) your own records of the activities currently available at the school and the impact they are having. Generally, however, it is likely that this information will already have been given to inspectors either as part of the SEF or in discussion with the school's senior leadership. However, you are entitled to submit information to an inspection team for their consideration. If you feel your school has a particularly strong ethos of parental involvement, you might want to help them 'blow their own trumpet'.

It is likely that inspectors will be particularly interested in the extent to which you are trying to engage 'hard-to-reach' parents. Do log the different attempts you have made and encourage your schools to do the same. 'Hard-to-reach' is exactly that and with the best will in the world there will be some who remain stubbornly distant. Where these are the parents of an excluded pupil or a vulnerable pupil, inspectors may be particularly interested to see what has been done to engage them.

Partnership work

Again, your partnership work is a vital part of the role. You might help your school by providing an up-to-date list of the active partnerships you are aware of. You will not be aware of all of them. Many of the teaching staff may be working with other schools in some form of partnership.

11 Is it working?

Chapter aims

- To identify different methods of checking on progress
- To explain how to use a baseline survey
- To provide you with some tools for creating your own surveys
- To understand the benefits and disadvantages of different types of interviews

Topics

- Evaluating your provision
- The baseline survey
- Creating your own surveys
- Interviews and discussions

Figures

Tables

Online resources

Gone are the days when you might have put something into operation and then stood back to see what happened. Now, setting your goals, targets or success criteria is essential, and identifying the means of measuring progress against them even more so. You are expected to demonstrate the value that your projects add and to be efficient in selecting your measurement tools.

Some aspects of identifying and measuring outcomes have been covered in Chapter 8. In this chapter, we focus on the checking of success for you and your schools rather than external funding sources.

Evaluating your provision

Having decided on the aims and outcomes of your project, it is important that you measure the progress of activities and how far you have achieved them. In order to do this, you will need to have created outcome indicators. These will allow you to measure progress towards your overall outcomes and the changes that have taken place. Table 11.1 provides some examples of outcomes and outcome indicators.

Table 11.1 Outcome indicators

Outcome	Outcome Indicator
Families with teenagers feel more able to handle behaviour and more supported	• Quantity of families attending parenting course • Parents state that they feel more able to cope • Level of contact parents have with other families • Level of contact parents have with other agencies

In order to work out whether your outcomes and outcome indicators have been achieved, you will need to gather information and evidence. This will include the views of participants, reports of their actions and the observations of staff. You can use a variety of tools including:

- baseline surveys
- data analysis
- records of observations
- focus groups
- surveys
- plenary sessions
- interviews
- discussions
- administrative records
- local area statistics
- audio recordings
- transcripts.

It is important to remember that monitoring attendance at activities will provide you with data, but this will not evaluate their quality. You will need to demonstrate clearly what the impact has been on participants and what they have done since.

One method of capturing the changes that have taken place is to use a baseline survey. This involves recording the views of your participants before they start the project, course or sessions and then taking a 'snapshot' midway through. Ask participants to complete a feedback form at the end of the course (see online resource 11.2) and, if possible, use a follow-up to participants after a period of 11.2
time. It is useful to collect information to demonstrate what they have done as a result of the course.

Using a baseline survey can help you adapt the project as you go along as you will see at an earlier stage whether it is achieving its aims or not. The more you are able to involve participants in the evaluation process, the more they will have an increased sense of ownership. Don't be put off by reluctance from providers to evaluate. They may see it as time-consuming or irrelevant or even feel threatened by the process. It is worth taking time to explain its importance and the fact that it is there to improve the service to meet the needs of participants.

The baseline survey

A baseline survey relies on you collecting evidence about the starting point of your participants. This is useful not only to show progress but also to give you a clear view of how confident participants are at the outset and what their expectations are.

Pre-course questions

Figure 11.1 provides some examples of pre-course questions. This is also available as online resource 11.1. 11.1

What are you expecting to get out of this course? What are your objectives?					
How would you describe your current understanding of the subject or activity?	None 1	 2	 3	 4	Extensive 5
What level of skills do you feel you have in this area?	Basic 1	 2	 3	 4	Advanced 5
How do you feel about taking part in this activity?	Nervous 1	 2	 3	 4	Comfortable 5
How do you expect the course to impact on your everyday life?	Little 1	 2	 3	 4	Wide 5

Figure 11.1 Pre-course survey

You can then use the information to check that your planned programme is appropriate for those participating. If, for example, your respondents are generally reporting that they are nervous about taking part, you might want to use the first sessions as a more gentle introduction to the course content with opportunity to chat, share experiences and get to know one another first. Of course, much will depend upon the time that is available and if you are working to a very strict and prescribed schedule this may be more difficult to do. However, what you don't want is to find that half of your participants don't turn up for session two!

It is also beneficial if participants see that you are taking their responses into consideration. This increases their level of involvement. So, for example, making reference to your baseline survey results in a general way and how you are using these to adapt course content will make individuals feel that it is worthwhile giving you their views. Some of those attending may have great apprehension about embarking on something new. They could have had difficulties at school and now have negative feelings about any type of course. They may have practical difficulties with reading and writing or retaining information. A priority for you, in these cases, is putting people at their ease.

Mid-course questions

You will need to decide at what point during your course it might be appropriate to check on progress. It should be a time where, if there are significant difficulties, you have enough remaining sessions to make some adjustments. Equally, it should not be so early that nothing has been achieved. Figure 11.2 provides some suggestions for questions you might include.

Is the course what you were expecting? Is it meeting your objectives?					
How would you describe your current understanding of the subject or activity?	None 1	 2	 3	 4	Extensive 5
What level of skills do you feel you have in this area?	Basic 1	 2	 3	 4	Advanced 5
How do you feel about taking part in this activity?	Nervous 1	 2	 3	 4	Comfortable 5
How do you expect the course to impact on your everyday life?	Little 1	 2	 3	 4	Wide 5

Figure 11.2 Baseline mid-point survey

Apart from the lead-in question, all the question are identical to those in the pre-course survey. This will enable you to see what progress is being made. When handing out the survey, you should explain clearly that you would like people to respond as they are feeling now. Are they as nervous? Do they know more? Have their skills improved?

If there are any difficulties spanning more than a couple of respondents (depending upon the size of your group), you might want to spend time adjusting the content of your course. If issues seem to be specifically related to one or two individuals, you will need to discuss these with each person.

End-of-course questions

Although this survey does not provide you with the opportunity to address any issues for the current cohort, it does provide useful summative evidence about the success of the course and can help you to adjust any future sessions. Figure 11.3 provides some suggestions for questions you might include (template available as online resource 11.2).

11.2

Think about the outcomes that you stated at the beginning of the course. In what way did the course meet the expectations or outcomes?	
What did you enjoy about the course?	
Is there anything that you did not enjoy?	
What did you learn? List three things.	1 2 3
How would you describe your understanding of the subject or activity?	None Extensive 1 2 3 4 5
What level of skills do you feel you have in this area?	Basic Advanced 1 2 3 4 5
How do you now feel about performing this activity?	Nervous Comfortable 1 2 3 4 5
How do you expect the course to impact on your everyday life?	Little Wide 1 2 3 4 5
What will you now do as a result of completing this activity or course?	

Figure 11.3 End-of-course survey

It is particularly beneficial if you are able to return to participants three to six months later to find out if there has been any sustained impact.

Having collected this information during the course of the project, you will want to collate the results for your own benefit, for any sponsors and possibly for Ofsted.

It is suggested that you total all the points for each question and then divide it by the number of participants. Using the average rather than the total number will give you a better idea of progress, particularly if the number of respondents has changed (Figure 11.4).

Aspect	**Average number of points – beginning of course**	**Average number of points – middle of course**	**Average number of points – end of course**
Understanding of the subject and activity			
Level of skill			
Feelings about taking part			
Impact on everyday life			

Figure 11.4 Survey results

Creating your own surveys

If you want to design a survey of your own, you need to consider the balance you wish to have between multiple choice and the use of scales or open-ended questions. The surveys above include both. This is beneficial as it provides respondents with the opportunity to write more extensively and expand on answers whilst also providing you with some data to demonstrate impact.

When drawing up questions try to:

- keep them short and to the point;
- avoid linking two questions together as one;
- avoid open-ended questions that will just elicit a yes/no answer;
- keep the main objectives in mind;
- keep the survey short – 10 minutes maximum for completion;
- craft them according to your need – use multiple choice and scales for demonstrating progress and open-ended questions to provide you with more detail;
- avoid jargon that participants might not understand;
- avoid sensitive or negative questions.

Figures 11.5–11.9 provide some examples of different formats you might use.

How do you rate the different sessions of the 'helping in school' course?	**Very good**	**Good**	**OK**	**Poor**	**Very poor**
Introduction					
School routines					
Confidentiality					
Jobs you might help with					
Letting us know					
Your questions					

Figure 11.5 Survey format 1

	Very effective	**Effective**	**Not effective**
How would you describe the teaching approach taken?			
How would you describe the individual study sessions?			

Figure 11.6 Survey format 2

Following the 'behaviour management course'	Always	Usually	Sometimes	Never
I feel more in control of my child's behaviour				
My child is behaving better at home				
My child is behaving better at school				

Figure 11.7 Survey format 3

Do you believe the behaviour management course has had a positive impact on your relationships with your child?		
Major impact	Some impact	No impact at all
☐	☐	☐

Figure 11.8 Survey format 4

Another way in which you might organize your questions is to ask the extent to which participants agree/disagree with selected statements (Figure 11.9).

Please tick	Strongly agree	Agree	Disagree	Strongly disagree
The course objectives have been met				
I have learnt how to use rewards and sanctions effectively				
The course has helped improve my relationship with my child				

Figure 11.9 Survey format 5

Interviews and discussions

Interviews can be a very useful method of following-up any particular issues that have come to light from your survey. For example, if you have a respondent who has made very little progress and they are willing to meet with you, you might want to discuss this further. Equally you might have participants who will find it difficult to complete a survey or you may just prefer to use a face-to-face approach. If you do, you will need to decide how formal you want the interview to be (Table 11.2).

Table 11.2 Interview formats

Type of interview	Advantages	Disadvantages
Group interview	Interviewees are more confident if there is several of them Quicker than doing individual interviews	Some interviewees may feel intimidated by others or allow more vocal individuals to lead the conversation
Informal discussion (group)	More likely to get open and honest comments on a variety of issues	Can be difficult to keep the focus Some people may dominate the conversation
Informal or semi-structured one-to-one interview	Can be more relaxed than using structured questions Can easily follow different lines of enquiry	Can be difficult to keep a focus Some people feel intimidated when being asked questions on their own
Structured one-to-one interview	Can keep a clear focus on particular questions Allows comparison between different interviewees	Is the most intimidating form of interview Can prevent exploration of emerging issues

Whichever type of interview you decide on, you will need to ask permission beforehand to record answers or make notes. If you decide to record the interview, you will need to write up the transcript afterwards. This can actually be quite a time-consuming and difficult activity. Taking notes at the same time as asking questions is quite a skill. An alternative is that you ask someone else to be present to make notes or take minutes.

The relationship you have with the participants can make a big difference to the way they answer questions. If you have been running or are closely involved in the provision, they may find it difficult to be open and honest in their responses. An alternative is to ask someone else to conduct the interview.

Forums and discussion groups are a much more informal and relaxed way of harnessing opinion. The dynamics of the group will make a big difference to the messages you are hearing. One, forceful individual with strong views can soon alter the whole balance and direction of responses. You need to skilfully bring the conversation back to your agenda and try to ensure that quieter members of the group have chance to give their opinion. If you suspect that someone has not felt able to share their views in this context, you might follow this up at a later date with the individual involved.

12 The School Improvement Planning Framework

Chapter aims

- To clarify what the School Improvement Planning Framework is
- To provide examples of some of the materials
- To provide guidance on how you might help your schools to use it

Topics

- The School Improvement Planning Framework
- Using the School Improvement Planning Framework
- Closing thoughts

Figures

Tables

Online resources

- 12.1 Extended services and ECM
- 12.2 Linking school priorities and the core offer
- 12.3 Extended services action plan – school priorities

Partnership working forms a large part of the extended services programme. For it to be truly effective, schools and agencies need to be able to work together with common goals for the good of the child. It sounds simple and it is common sense; however, it is not that easy to apply.

Agencies have worked apart for too long. Many are still entrenched in their own philosophies and practices and are reluctant to truly 'merge' with one another. The top-down blending into 'Children's services' has not been an easy transition. Calling something by a different name does not necessarily alter the outlook of its participants.

Another major impediment is the standards agenda. Whilst schools are expected to be exclusively focused upon standards, the ECM agenda and extended services will not be a priority. We are a long way from the majority of schools being prepared to truly acknowledge their central role in supporting the development of the whole child and the child's family. Some schools still see themselves as an academic bastion and feel that they are being asked to take on aspects of support and partnership working that really are nothing to do with them. This is further compounded by the government's emphasis on league tables, accountability and target-setting. Only when this emphasis is relinquished will schools truly feel able to concentrate on the level of need amongst all their students and not just those on borderline grades.

Schools and partner agencies need to be able to share a vision that takes them away from their own individual agendas towards one for the community. The extended services coordinator should have a key role in working with schools on their improvement plans to enable a balance of activities across the cluster (see online resource 12.1 'Extended services and ECM'). At the moment, schools can be reluctant to share their school improvement plans and self-evaluation 12.1

12.2 & 12.3

forms at all. This is a pity as sharing relevant areas from a school's plan with the ESC enables him/her to inform the cluster and individual school development plan. Extended services and school improvement planning should be one agenda. Online resources 12.2 'Linking school priorities and the core offer' and 12.3 'Extended services action plan – school priorities' could be used to highlight school priorities and provide suggested actions.

The School Improvement Planning Framework (SIPF) goes some way towards encouraging schools and their partners to work in a more collaborative sense towards shared goals – the ECM outcomes for every child.

The School Improvement Planning Framework

The School Improvement Planning Framework (SIPF) was originally published in 2007 by the Training and Development Agency (TDA). Since then an amended version was published in 2008. The purpose of the framework is to assist schools in planning not only their own priorities but also ways in which they can support those of the local community. Although still with the ultimate aim of improving standards of attainment and the well-being of pupils, it acknowledges that other factors in pupils' lives have an impact on school priorities.

The framework can be ordered from the website www.tda.gov.uk.

As shown in Table 12.1, the framework consists of the following modules:

- prepare and engage
- inside the classrooms
- learning potential
- beyond the classroom
- personalize
- develop and prioritize solutions
- plan delivery and evaluation.

Table 12.1 SIPF model

Prepare and engage	**Identify objectives**	**Ensure successful outcomes**	
	Inside the classroom	Personalize	
	Learning potential	Develop and prioritize solutions	Plan delivery and evaluation
	Beyond the classroom		

There are therefore three stages in the planning process:

1 Prepare and engage – creating a planning process that takes into account where you are now, what you want to achieve and the methods you are going to use to plan this.
2 Identify objectives:
   - inside the classroom – setting objectives to improve teaching and learning that take pupil well-being into account;
   - learning potential – the factors and barriers that affect the potential of pupils to learn and how they might be overcome;
   - beyond the classroom – ways of improving the well-being of all pupils in the school and community through extended services.
3 Ensure successful outcomes:
   - personalize – assess the needs of targeted individuals or groups;
   - develop and prioritize solutions – to help meet school improvement objectives;
   - plan delivery and evaluation – create a practical and achievable plan for implementation.

Using the School Improvement Planning Framework

It is up to the schools themselves to select from the materials in the SIPF. What they choose, if anything, will depend upon their own stage of development in terms of ECM and extended services. However, there are some materials that you might draw their attention to.

Diagnosing where you are

The SIPF materials encourage schools to think about the extent to which they involve stakeholders in the improvement planning process. Schools can be very precious about their improvement planning; however, the duty to promote community cohesion is an incentive to encourage them to reflect on the level of involvement that different groups have. They might ask the following questions:

- Who is involved in the process of developing our school improvement plan?
- Who takes the lead in our planning process?
- What is the scope of our school improvement plan?
- How is the well-being of all pupils integrated into the plan?
- Does the plan support personalized learning?
- What type of objectives are set?
- To what extent are successful outcomes evidenced?
- Is there a feedback process that informs future plans?

Who should be involved?

Although you will already have done some detailed research into who your agencies, contacts and local groups are, your schools may still have only a partial understanding of the real network they are part of.

The SIPF encourages schools to reflect on who should be involved in the planning process and who should make up wider stakeholder group. Schools usually already involve governors, parents, pupils and staff but to what extent are other stakeholders involved? The SIPF materials identify three stages of involvement:

- Are actively involved in the planning process.
- Provide input through consultation to the process.
- Will need to be informed of your plans.

Not all agencies need to be or should be actively involved. Some will just need to be informed. However, consideration should be given to what is desirable even if there is a long way to go. Schools might want to use the format in Figure 12.1 to record their thoughts.

Type of stakeholder	Who they are	The extent to which they are currently involved	How they might be involved further
Whole-school workforce			
Senior leadership team			
Pupils			
Parents			
Extended services cluster manager			
Parent support adviser			
School improvement partners			
Children's centres			
Nurseries			
Health services			
Social care services			
Extended services cluster schools			
Voluntary organizations			
Agency partners			
Local authority extended services leads			
Other agencies			
Other local authority teams			

Figure 12.1 Stakeholder involvement

What's working?

The SIPF provides a variety of materials to encourage schools to reflect on their current practice within and beyond the classroom. This includes the traditional SWOT exercise (Figure 12.2) which might be used with other stakeholders to provide a different perspective on the opportunities and threats facing the school. Other services might possibly be aware of opportunities and threats within the environment that the school is not.

Strengths	Weaknesses
Opportunities	**Threats**

Figure 12.2 SWOT exercise

After completion of the SWOT, the following questions might be considered:

- How can we best exploit our strengths?
- How can we address our weaknesses effectively?
- How can we ensure we take advantage of our opportunities?
- How can we anticipate threats and develop strategies for turning them into opportunities?
- Are any of the responses surprising?

The results can be used to inform the rest of the improvement planning process.

Through using the material 'What's working' and the 'Five whys', the framework encourages participants to identify aspects of school provision that are:

- working well
- working so so
- not working well.

From here it is suggested that schools consider five 'whys' as to the reasons behind the success and failure of different projects.

Identifying barriers

This section of the SIPF aims to identify the factors that affect pupils' learning potential and well-being in the school. It includes the following questions:

- What are the key characteristics of successful learners?
- Why don't some pupils exhibit these characteristics?
- What are the enablers and blockers to pupils' learning?
- What aims need to be developed as a result of identifying the blockers?
- What activities can help make progress towards these aims?

Schools might use the flow chart in Figure 12.3 to help them cover and record these steps.

What are the key characteristics of successful learners?
e g. takes risks, asks questions, reflects on their learning

↓

Blockers	Enablers
e.g. boring curriculum, lack of parental expectations	e.g. good home routine, experience of success

↓

Positive aims
e.g. provide opportunities for all children to experience success develop effective family partnerships

↓

Your aim	Existing activities	Potential activities
Provide opportunities to experience success	Varied range of activities available	Study support Intercultural activities including music and drama

Figure 12.3 Identifying barriers

ECM sort cards

It is intended that schools use these sort cards (Figure 12.4) to help work out what their priorities might be. The activity involves schools placing the cards on a grid (Figure 12.5).

1 Being healthy	2 Staying safe	3 Enjoying and achieving	4 Making a positive contribution	5 Achieving economic well-being
Parents, carers and families promote healthy choices	Parents, carers and families provide safe homes and stability	Parents, carers and families support learning	Parents, carers and families promote positive behaviour	Parent, carers and families are supported to be economically active
Physically healthy	Safe from maltreatment, neglect, violence and sexual exploitation	Ready for school	Engage in decision making and support the community and environment	Engage in further education, employment or training on leaving school
Mentally and emotionally healthy	Safe from accidental injury and death	Attend and enjoy school	Engage in law-abiding and positive behaviour in and out of school	Ready for employment
Sexually healthy	Safe from bullying and discrimination	Achieve stretching national educational standards at primary school	Develop positive relationships and choose not to bully or discriminate	Live in decent homes and sustainable communities
Live healthy lifestyles	Safe from crime and anti-social behaviour in and out of school	Achieve personal and social development and enjoy recreation	Develop self-confidence and successfully deal with significant life changes and challenges	Have access to transport and material goods
Choose not to take illegal drugs	Have security, stability and be cared for	Achieve stretching national educational standards at secondary school	Develop enterprising behaviour	Live in households free from low income

Figure 12.4 ECM sort cards

Using a grid staff can work together to place the cards according to:

- the potential impact on pupils' life outcomes
- the school's ability to influence them.

The cards that are placed in the top right-hand corner should become priorities for the school. The cards that are placed in the bottom right hand corner should be possible aims for partner agencies.

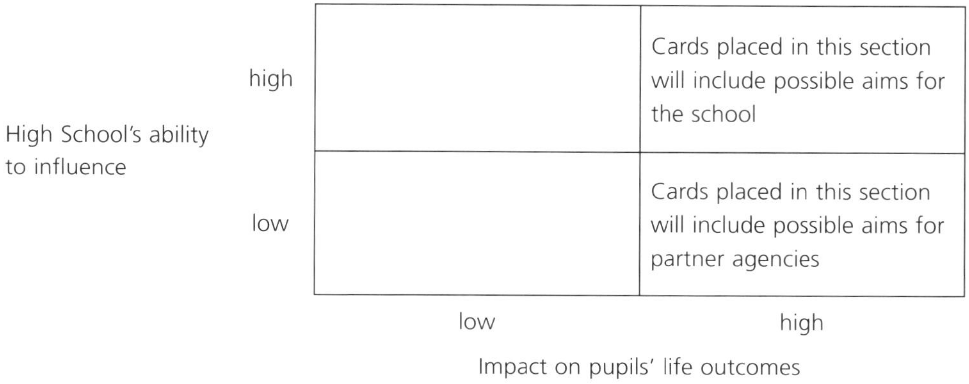

Figure 12.5 Sort card grid

This activity provides a good opportunity for partner services and school staff to work together with the ECM outcomes as the focus. Not only does it draw attention to the aims of ECM but it also highlights what each service can do to help. None of the aims are the exclusive business of one service. Every aim is a joint responsibility to achieve regardless of the high or low level of ability to influence.

Schools might try the activity as part of a staff meeting with the ESC present or be even more ambitious and use it for an INSET day inviting representatives from other agencies to work alongside school staff in groups. This, in itself could be an excellent opportunity to begin to understand the commonalities and differences. The networking done by the ECS in the community can be helpful to identify providers or services as they are highlighted in this exercise. This can be particularly beneficial in relation to services where schools feel they have little influence, such as housing.

Closing thoughts

We are concluding this book with a chapter on the SIPF because of its own strategic importance. The provision of extended services that support individuals and groups within the community is an enormously valuable and important development. We might feel that families should be able to cope and look after one another, that children should be supported and trouble-free and that we should all get on with our main business. The fact remains that they can't, they aren't and the 'main business' soon loses direction when chaotic home circumstances impede the organization's every effort.

The difficulty is that much of the extended services agenda has been 'applied' top-down and those receiving it are struggling to implement very laudable objectives in a structure and ethos that isn't quite ready for it. Of course, many people are doing many wonderful things and successfully bend, manipulate and find a way to do most of what is expected. However, it is not until we all suspend our own targets and individual aspirations and work truly with the interests of the community in mind that real extended services will exist. And perhaps at this point they won't be extended at all but the real core offer for all children's services.

References

DCSF (2007) *Guidance on the Duty to Promote Community Cohesion* Nottingham: DCSF

DCSF (2006) *A guide to inter-agency working to safeguard and promote the welfare of children* London: TSO

DfES (2002b) *Extended Schools: Providing Opportunities and Services for All* London: DfES

DfES (2004) *Every Child Matters: Change for Children* London: DfES

DfES (2005) *Extended Schools: Access to Opportunities and Services for All: A prospectus* London: DfES

Ofsted (2008) 'Inspecting maintained schools' duty to promote community cohesion: guidance for inspectors' DCSF

Plowden Report (1967)'*Children and their Primary Schools'* London: HMSO

TDA (2008) *School Improvement Planning Framework* London: TDA

TDA website, www.tda.gov.uk

Index